THE FEMINISTS

By James E. Joyce

Printed in the United States of America
THE FEMINISTS

CONTENT

FORWARD

Any woman, not to mention any man, who refuses to analytically evaluate the information contained within this book, is simply a follower of unsubstantiated ridiculous dogma that contributes greatly to this country's moral decay. The truth will set you free as a responsible and independent thinker.

Absurdly, men have stood around for the well over a hundred years and observed the unfolding of one of the greatest tragedies of the twentieth century. It all began in earnestness in the late 1800's and has more than once brought the world to the brink of nuclear annihilation.

American FEMINISTS do not stand alone in responsibility for the world's present precarious situation. But it is time that they learn to accept a major share of the responsibility because of greedily pursuing the instincts of their male dominated personalities and listening to the sirens of their delicious fantasy world, thus leading the way, through negligence, to an amoral world.

Had American FEMINISTS followed the path of their feminine natures, utilizing the analytical skills of their masculine personas, we might be much closer to paradise on earth rather than the Faustian nightmare waiting just around the corner.

How did American FEMINISTS bring the country to this sorry state of affairs, and can the direction of their misguided selfishness be altered? The compelling reason for the vicious attack this book launches on the American FEMINIST, in all her various guises, is that she deserves it!

Over fifty years ago, a new wave of FEMINISTS began to spread throughout the country. Three fearless leaders published books that led millions of American women to jump off the cliff of life.

"NOW" in their own words will be revealed the utter nonsense that permeated the pages of their diatribes.

Note:

Throughout the book the reader will encounter many direct quotations from various sources. Within these quotations will be found the omission identifier ". . ." These omissions within the context of the quotations are simply a means for simplifying the length of the quoted information. Such exclusion within the quotation does not change the validity of the quote. The reader can verify the accuracy of the previous statement by referring to the original works quoted.

Occasionally, portions of the quoted material will be underlined and/or highlighted to reinforce the absurdness of its originator's thought process or lack thereof.

I. "THE FEMALE EUNUCH"

The book by Germaine Greer is well written, filled with clever questions with no attempt at solutions. It's an excellent example of the confusion permeating the <u>New</u> Wave FEMINIST movement; <u>New</u> being distinguished from old only by chronology. There no appreciable difference in enlightenment.

Much to her credit, Germaine doesn't attempt to hide the fact of total ignorance and lack of meaningful direction epitomized by such statements as, "Revolution <u>ought</u> to entail the correction of some of the false perspectives which our assumptions about womanhood, sex, love, and society have combined to create." I have stressed the word <u>ought</u>. Germaine by her own admission has <u>no solutions</u>, only an intellectual stream of words.

According to her definition of the FEMINIST revolution, there isn't one, only chaos! "Revolution does little more than peep to what it would." The frustration and subconscious hatred within the FEMINIST liberators simply attempts to destroy the fabric of any social structure. These sorry, bitchy FEMINISTS entwine us all in a useless, perpetual cycle of emancipations and new beginnings.

Germaine goes on to reiterate the whining, tired, old literary quotation which has become mandatory FEMINIST reading in frivolous thought.

The heroine Nora asks Helmer (fictionally, over a hundred years ago), "What do you consider my most sacred duty?" Poor old Helmer being a tool in the hands of the author replies, "Your duty is to your husband and your children." The hip, chic author of that day sets up the punch line to be delivered by Nora, our 100-year-old smart ass, "I have another duty just as sacred . . . to myself"

Nora failed to tell the poor bastard this when she enticed him under her skirts, cloaked herself in his protection and married the poor devil. No doubt, she ever after nagged him to death about her impoverished state of slavery.

There is a strain of undeniable sadness and foreboding in Germaine's litany of endless words searching for meaning, "A feminist elite might seek to lead uncomprehending women in another arbitrary direction, training them as a task force in a battle that might, that <u>ought</u> never, to eventuate." Again we are reminded of the mindlessness of the 'ought' phrase.

Germaine then commits the unpardonable sin of reaching a conclusion and it is, of course, entirely fallacious! Conclusions and solutions to problems are to be religiously avoided; sacred no-no's in the worn out volumes of verbiage spewed forth from the bankrupt brains of the FEMINIST elitists.

So sure are these FEMINISTS **of their <u>Communist</u> beliefs** that Germaine comes to the same false conclusion in her book as will Friedan in hers. "The political conservatives ought to object that by advocating the destruction of the patterns of consumption carried out by the chief spenders, the housewives, the economy would collapse". Her book invites depression and hardship. **In other words enlightened American** FEMINISTS **will not buy things!**

This is tantamount to admitting that the oppression of housewives is necessary to the maintenance of the economy. Friedan reveled in her similarly predicted outcome. Germaine has a real feeling of concern because she believed it to be true.

Following the idiotic advice of their brilliant FEMINIST leaders, American FEMINISTS have entered the work force by the millions. As any man could have easily predicted, **all these** **FEMINISTS have become the biggest spenders and the** **greatest consumers in the history of the world**!

So much for the selflessness of the FEMINISTS and their shared stupid conclusion that FEMINISTS, if given the choice and independence, would be non-consumers. **What a bunch of goof balls!**

FEMINISTS convinced men that governments would be saner and wars simply unthinkable because of the political power of the enlightened FEMINIST voters. The same revolutionary rhetoric gave us prohibition, which of course resulted in a nation of alcoholics.

The need for medical attention grips the hearts of most FEMINISTS. By the millions, they became hooked on uppers and downers. Doctor, my husband doesn't understand me . . . doctor, I have these constant recurring headaches . . . doctor, I need this, give me that . . . I can't cope. Pills and more pills, if a doctor fails to acquiesce to these demands, he is persona grata with the girls. When all the doctors caved in and gave them what they wanted, it was the doctors who were manipulating them, the poor little; innocent American FEMINISTS were duped again.

False, sweeping generalizations, applied with gospel like evangelism by FEMINISTS often hook them a group of weak minded men, who sheepishly go along with these utterly silly, insipid mental delusions. Of course, the same men back the stand of FEMINISTS with regard to abortion because they can get all the sex they want without accepting the responsibility of fatherhood.

What do such cruel hoaxes perpetrated on the public have to do with Germaine's incisive observation, that given their economic freedom, FEMINISTS would destroy capitalism?

Because not only is capitalism archaic, but American Women invented consumerism! Who is trying to kid whom? Consumerism thrives on the American FEMINISTS constant, unrelenting dissatisfaction.

Early quotations in Germaine's book and her other musings emphasize a complete preoccupation with self. The verbal juggling acts that she attempts boggle the mind.

First She declares self-interest as one of her prerequisite necessities. Her attempt at combining self interest with altruism collapses through the utterings of her own penmanship.

Germaine's and, I suspect, millions of other FEMINISTS' mental neuroses are summarily verbalized, "... **my fantasy is that it might be possible to leap the steps of revolution and arrive at liberty and <u>communism</u> without strategy or revolutionary discipline.**"

Miss Greer's simultaneous embrace of selfishness, liberty and Communism without the necessity of discipline, strategy or revolution aptly describes the mental and emotional aberrations of a singularly confused personality. SUCH ALSO IS THE STATE OF BEING OF AMERICAN FEMINISTS!

FEMINISTS need is to be loved, not give love. They demand freedom to fantasize, not engage in life. Their desire is to be communal in the appearance of caring without self-discipline. They refuse to accept the consequences of their actions. They refuse either out of selfishness or ignorance to alter their false personalities to correspond to essence. This is the fantasy world in which American FEMINISTS reside.

Communism, granting the articulate but utterly confused Germaine every possible latitude of definitions, spans the description of Russian totalitarianism to the kindest form of human endeavors attributed to the teachings of Jesus Christ. The many gratifications of self and liberty are the very antithesis of Communism. The measure of ultimate FEMINIST altruism is the self-sacrifice of one FEMINIST'S life for another FEMINIST.

Having read the musings of Germaine, it is apparent that no one who remains a FEMINIST actually read her book or, as often is the case, can read with any penetration of the cranial cortex. **The dichotomies of irrational argument thus far addressed filled only the first twelve pages of the introduction to her book.**

II. GLORIA
"IN EXCELSUS" STEINEM

In Alfred Hitchcock's film, "The Trouble with Harry", we knew that Harry was dead. **"Outrageous Acts and Everyday Rebellions"** by Steinem creates the illusion that there really is a Gloria and that she believes passionately in something.

Her rambling tidbits and self-effacements vesselize a room with volumes of hot air, megabytes of verbiage spewed forth from a clever mind desperately attempting to protect her self-knowledge of emptiness from public disclosure, while succumbing to the dream of authorship.

Such inner emptiness could explain why there was never any depth or length to her "ARTICLES". When the totality of her "career" was finally summarized in a single printing, the real Gloria surfaced and no one was there.

Her lack of presence makes the reader totally uncomfortable throughout the reading of her book. But then of course, how many FEMINISTS **have actually read the book**?

Germaine was flirting with intelligence and even in disagreement, feel her misguided enthusiasm for the FEMINIST'S movement.

Gloria is indeed a cat of a different stripe and her own worst enemy. Being unable to resist the limelight she hides as best she can from her true self, afraid of being found, wanting in integrity and substance. If one constructs a persona of vapor, one cannot be held and in turn, cannot hold another. thus she becomes neurotically untouchable, a "Cause Celebrate". To such a persona, fear of discovery is an obsession. Clever people of this nature conceal themselves in the open where they cannot be found.

Gloria, in all honesty, should be pitied, except that her vulnerability is, like so many of her kind, shielded by a rapier like clever mind which simply destroys all that is hostile to her security. In reading her book, finding nothing of substance, I became absolutely fascinated by the inescapable conclusion that GLORIA is a reflection and personification of all the left wing, empty headedness of American Liberal Causes!

Junk pseudo-intellectual verbiage, fostered on the public by the "Great Educated Minds" of the liberal arts and so-called intellectuals of the eastern establishment, is what knits together the publishing empires, the TV networks, the commentators and the banking community of BIG APPLE country.

It is one thing to titillate the minds of housewives or teenage girls in Oklahoma or Kansas, but when you get the feeling that these people really believe what they are doing, it's very scary. The more they profess to know, the scarier it becomes. This is exactly what Gloria's best seller tells us.

Perhaps, I am the only one who actually read her "BOOK". After perusing pages 9 through 26, one simply cannot take the girl seriously; One wonders at the publishing house that would put its name to such nonsense. Gloria refers to herself **220 times** in the first person singular, "I", **in just those 18 pages**.

It quickly becomes apparent that here is one hell of an insecure human being. On page 20 in a brief paragraph she refers to herself no less than ten times, on page 26, nine times in six lines and on page 12, three times in a single line.

The "I's" were counted because there was nothing worthwhile to take the reader's mind off of Gloria, and the poor reader is only in the introduction of the book.

Gloria is a clever little thing; finally, subconsciously, later in the book, she must recognize the shallowness of herself. Out of nowhere she references the egotism of males by their constant evocation of the first person singular, I, in their speech and writing patterns.

Gloria goes on to caveat herself and other FEMINISTS as exceptions to this type of aggrandizement by informing us that when writing, women personalize their experience and as such are not seekers of power but transmitters of their true emotions to one another. Such a line of crap can come only from the most insecure of personalities.

After completion of the "I, Gloria" counts, I reflected upon the utter selfishness of these FEMINISTS. It became my only salvation. The message of FEMINISM is SELF, I, ME, MINE and TRIVIA of thought. An airhead pretense to seduce both women and stupid men (that's the easy part) that there is something profound to be learned in the halls of academia. The same old garbage is being sold and repackaged year after year to new gullibles.

Trivia is all we have to deal with, so look out trivia! Here we come. Page 35, "I Was a Playboy Bunny", Gloria's big expose in the nineteen sixties that catapulted her to fame. She recounts how clever she was, "fabricated and typed" a personal history. Euphemistically Gloria means **she lied and falsified an employment record.**

Nice girl, typical New York reporter, she protects us from dirty politicians and lying corporate executives. Just the type of left wing FEMINIST champion you and I can admire for her brilliant journalism. Perhaps, perish the thought; Gloria was interested in earning a little bread and notoriety. Naturally her sterling acts of outrageous rebellion protect us from the likes of L. B. J. and Richard Nixon.

Steinem shames the men who run PLAYBOY. These animals are users of innocent young women. We know because Gloria tells us so. Old Glo can't help jiving us when revealing an intimate conversation she had on page 55 with another bunny one evening,

"You're better at serving drinks and getting the jerks out fast." Now who is really using whom? Come on Glo, you must be writing for infantile FEMINIST mentalities.

In defense of women there are heartfelt words spoken about long hours, low pay and boredom. On page 69, she recounts the long-term effects the Bunny Article had upon her. "There was the realization that all women are bunnies, among the long term results of this article . . . Realizing that all women are Bunnies, since FEMINISM, I've finally stopped regretting I wrote the article."

Gloria wishes to somehow assure her place in the history book of crazy causes. In her book, she relates how through ill timing and misfortune in the middle 1960's we were deprived of the great political mind of John Kenneth Galbraith. You may recall that this Harvard professor of economics was appointed by John F. Kennedy as Ambassador to India, another of the President's minor miscalculations.

Page 70, the year is 1965 and the air is filled with excitement. Gloria is invited by Galbraith (and she takes pains to note, his family) to attend a very important weekend rendezvous at Big John's place. She was invited, even though at the time she was hardly a household word in journalism together with another patsy, Senator George McGovern.

Present at the meeting were Arthur Schlesinger Jr., other members of the old Kennedy administration and a number of Harvard "scholars". These giants of the eastern establishment conversed on the heart rendering topics of our time . . . draft resistant movement is beginning . . . anything to avoid killing and getting killed in this immoral war

Kennedy had put 17,000 combat troops in Vietnam. He also concurred with the CIA on the necessity of ridding itself of the cumbersome president of South Vietnam, and in his spare time handed Cuba to the Russians on a silver platter. All of these grand achievements were accomplished with the comfort and advice of the people in that very room.

The plan at the meeting was, of course, to disavow any connection with such stupid policies. It was very simple, spread the word, it was all the doing of that dumb Texan in the White House, L. B. J.

Three years after inheriting the Kennedy mess, he was the obvious evil monster. Johnson made enough mistakes of his own; he didn't have to also account for Kennedy's!

Almost in the same breath, old Glo puts in a plug for her mentor to be, George McGovern, "In 1964 while other politicians were still lamenting 'the Negro problem' McGovern, then a freshman senator, was condemning 'white racism'." Not a bad idea if you've bigger political fish to fry and by the way just how many Americans Negroes are there in North Dakota?

Gloria sums up the character, fortitude and genius of these intrepid, pioneer stock, eastern elite by relating an exciting vignette of their shared heroism and intellectual creativity. Honest to God folks it's all there in her book; so ridiculous that it shall forever remain a shining symbol of FEMINISM at its best.

The tale begins on page 73, as Gloria writes, "I began to understand that he shares my problem: he's great in emergencies but can't handle everyday life." In the described scene that follows, it turns out that brave George, about to leave with Gloria in tow, at the conclusion of the weekend meetings, discovers he has left the key in the rent-a-car's ignition and to boot, in the <u>ON</u> position. The battery is dead.

Gloria proceeds to describe how big John Galbraith, ex-ambassador, Harvard renowned economist, comes to the gallant rescue. The consensus of the three adventurers is that Galbraith will, with his trusty automobile, shove the rent-a-car, carrying Glo and George, not several hundred feet, but over dirty, dusty back roads to the nearest garage.

It is truly a scene straight out of a Marx brothers' comedy; better suited to "THREE'S COMPANY" than that of a kingmaker and a future presidential candidate. The brilliant kingmaker and "err" apparent to the Kennedy myth is banging along a dirt road, pushing and bumping a battery dead rent-a-car, in which are encapsulated a future Democratic presidential candidate and one of the great leaders of the American FEMINIST Movement. Thrilling episode, what!

Obviously there were no phones on the premises and no jumper cables in any of the other vehicles. Must have been an automatic transmission, otherwise the car would have started with a relatively small push. Of course, if it were an automatic transmission, then certainly the three wise eggheads would have known not to have it pushed while in gear. Galbraith must love, beyond measure, slamming into the back of a rent-a-car traveling in neutral gear over bumpy, hilly, back roads.

Is it any wonder the damn federal government is a sick joke, when people of this level of incompetence in everyday life are advisors and participators in world decision-making processes? There are of course numerous simple solutions to such a minor inconvenience.

For instance, big John could have driven to the garage and brought back a set of jumper cables. FREE TICKETS to the next "NOW" meeting and a Ph.D. in Economics from Harvard University for anyone who comes up with another easy solution.

The next time you hear of a proposal from anyone in government regarding a solution to a problem, just recall Gloria's tale about the three mental giants beating the hell out of two automobiles; one pushing the other along miles of country roads. Galbraith must have arrived at this unique solution while in India.

Our intrepid crisis survivors, Gloria and George, just went along for the ride. But wait! Don't take my word for it; go to the library (free), it's all there in black and white, page 73. Hold on, that's only half the story! Elsewhere in the folds of her book is the quotation that led Gloria to becoming George's 1972 ad hoc press secretary.

Right there is her description as to George's determination to start a car with a dead battery by turning on the key and stepping on the gas pedal, ". . . stubborn, tenacious, dogged the way he went about trying to start a car . . . he just didn't give up." I'm not kidding; it's all there. Believe it or Not!

Most people would call such behavior STUPID, but then in the topsy-turvy world of American FEMINISTS, vices are virtues and vice versa. God! These people are just plain dumb and have the education to prove it. Either that or Old Glo missed her true calling as a great comedic sketch writer. A fiery revolutionary, Smith girl, bless her little heart. She came straight from the intellectual furnaces of a great liberal college. Glo came from the arts, humanities, literature genre of graduates; well bred, well spoken, well read and nothing but air between the ears.

Gloria continues to fascinate her adoring readership (coffee table display purchasers) as breathlessly she summons up her belief in McGovern's integrity, "I wonder how this unpretentious, honest man became a politician." Tha . . . tha . . . tha . . . that's all folks! Her idea of another great man was John Lindsay, "electing a mayor who can and will go to the neighborhoods of the poor."

Of course he did Gloria and then like all good politicians he went back to his wealthy upper New York pad and lived happily ever after. In her book, our little, unbiased reporter writes about Lindsay's fearless trip to the New York slums. Later, we will compare this breathless, hero worshipping description of Lindsay with a similar trip by Richard Nixon in which Gloria vilifies this poor man.

Gloria absolutely adores Eugene McCarthy, at least on page 79,   ". . . he was an intellectual, a teacher . . ." Yeah, Glo! He was also a politician, amateur poet and ex-baseball player. A teacher by definition does not necessarily an intellectual make. Later, on page 81 she recants, giving up on both Bobby Kennedy and McCarthy when all her friends began taking sides in the 1968 presidential primaries," . . . friends no longer spoke to friends, and common goals were forgotten. Gossip about who had switched to whom politically was suddenly as juicy as who was having an affair with whom."

Either Gloria, out of her own mouth, is a silly Pollyanna or is still writing high school teasers for the illiterate. Later, she reverses her opinion about Robert Kennedy when she interviews Caesar Chavez. Chavez tells her that Kennedy has ambassador credentials with the black nation within this nation.

Gloria's "Journalism" has all the trite phrases of a true romance novel and not half the fun. Her prose is lacking in humor and is coupled with a constantly changing mentality; indicating a lack of strong, forceful character, hardly one chosen to lead a revolution of profound righteousness.

Her Lack of integrity is further attested to on page 91. "I was designated to become a kind of Manchurian candidate on the Nixon campaign plane . . . who reports not the respectful, circumspect news . . . but Nixon's behavior . . ." Glo is a great gal, always willing to snitch and snoop under the protective title of "Journalist". Worse yet, what she turns up is innocuous junk and she believes she is another Mata Hari.

I'm somewhat committed to continuing with a critique of her totally worthless book. It should be classified as having no redeeming social value, right along side kiddy porn. If by now you have had enough, believe me it only gets more embarrassing as it continues. Do yourself a favor and skip to Chapter IV, although by then you may wish to throw up.

Remember that these are the ninnies who convinced American Women to leave their homes, abort over one million babies a year and encourage women to commit economic suicide. There is nothing of substance in Gloria's entire novelette and we're only on page 91.

For those with strong stomachs let us continue. Back a page or two I asked you to keep in mind Gloria's fawning report of John Lindsay's visit to the New York slums. In her eyes, Lindsay was a courageous and utterly handsome man. Now on pages 94 and 95 she describes an almost identical visit by Richard Nixon to a black neighborhood.

". . . rubbed his sweating palms together." Then referring to the same visit, ". . . in this well oiled campaign, Nixon stayed in his gold and white French provincial apartment . . . surrounded by gifts from famous people . . ."

Obviously either Lindsay was shrewd enough not to let this silly little broad into his New York mansion or he was poor as a church mouse. Bless her little heart; I do believe Glo used her credentials to manage the news? If by now you are not fed up with this dolly's petty na, na, na then you are a candidate for sucker of the week on her FEMINIST dance card.

To get the unpretentious, honest McGovern elected, Gloria Steinem did some really neat things, "I actually went out and bought covered-up, mud colored clothes . . ." Terrific! Big City Smith FEMINIST shucks down-home country bumpkins and laughs it up back in the "Big Apple". As written, either her disclosures are a form of literary suicide or a subconscious plea for restoration as a responsible member of the human race.

Steinem became enraged over an incident in which George McGovern was told by Abe Ribicoff, a potential financial backer, that no broads would be allowed at a meeting to discuss Ribicoff's backing of McGovern for a run at the presidency. To such a rebuff Gloria sarcastically remarks, "McGovern, for instance, would never have let Ribicoff get away with saying, 'No blacks or Jews'. No broads was somehow acceptable."

This incident is described between pages 110 and 116 in her book. Being the red-blooded FEMINIST she is, did old Glo march upon old Ribicoff and demand satisfaction? No, she blamed George.

I hate to disillusion little Glo. Quite honestly, any politician worth his salt would have excluded George Washington, Abe Lincoln or Jesus Christ if he wanted Ribicoff's money for the quest of a lifetime. Hey Gloria, by the way isn't Ribicoff Jewish?

Steinem the fearless FEMINIST leader finally gets down to the nitty-gritty. She confirms the necessity for women to accept full responsibility for their children. "So the right to reproductive freedom will be raised at the convention anyway."

FEMINISTS need to be reminded that such freedom of choice also entails the responsibility to their husbands for the child's upkeep.

If the father is not included in the mother's decision making process to bear a child, and if the woman chooses not to abort, then she is responsible for all costs, care and nurturing of that child. Correspondingly, if she aborts the baby then she must bear whatever pain, mental anguish and possible God punishment in later life and after death that awaits her. She can be certain of one thing; old Glo won't lose any sleep over her anguish.

The central section of Steinem's book gets rolling on sisterhood; the homogeny of overworked women; devoid of power, stuck with rearing children and treated like servants. Men, she whines . . . now get this ". . . have someplace to go - the bars, a street corner, someplace to get together."

Women mind you, according to Steinem, have no place but their homes and their families and are therefore isolated from other females. This, my friends, is a very sick mind at work, an addlebrained menace to society.

Gloria is ecstatic about a creative solution concocted by FEMINISTS to resolve **their domestic maid problem**!

These brilliant, incisive women, in one evening, accomplished the singularly great achievement of ridding females of the domination of men forever. Now look folks honest to God I'm not making all this stuff up, Gloria is proud of these things. She goes on to tell how one housewife organized a support group of white women who would extract from their husbands a living wage **for the FEMINISTS' domestic servants!** If this requires explanation, you are truly a "NOW GIRL". These pampered little creatures are twits; parasites on the good nature of all honest, hard working men and women.

How about page 117 on women, ". . . first in work or in war . . . and must serve as docile, unpaid or underpaid labor." or ". . . inside the white male club." One recalls Steinem's heroism down those dirty country roads in that fearsome old rent-a-car.

When she further expounds, "I have met brave women who are exploring the outer edge of human possibility . . ." I suspect that Steinem happened into a supermarket one day in between "ARTICLES" and found real women shopping for groceries. It does blow one's mind at the very thought, all of these brave women . . . the infinite universe!

But wait, there is eternal hope and Gloria, according to a quotation on page 118, may yet save mankind, "I'm just beginning, just beginning, to find out who I am." Keep looking Gloria, you are out there someplace! For all our sakes, may you someday find yourself. At thirty-four (then) you are at least making an effort. After all, nobody's perfect.

Gloria attempts to assign sainthood to an infamous Smith graduate, a convicted murderess. "Jean Harris's years of willing humiliation were laid bare by the press." Only Smith girls can take a convicted and confessed murderess and come up with a modern day Joan of Arc. When these gals don't get what they want, they become very vindictive, vicious and self-destructive. These are women of style without a shred of substance.

Speaking on behalf of the Smith class of '56 on page 121, ". . . families mean support and audience for men. To women they just mean work." There you have it ladies. When the poor little FEMINISTS of Smith run out of wealthy men and their yachts, the poor things, silly boobs (No girls, refer to Webster's on this one) go and conscript poor and frustrated women in order to punish men for something that hibernates unhealthy within their own FEMINIST selves. An apt medical description of their malady might be categorized as the IMEMINE disease.

I apologize to the readers who have continued to read on in this chapter after my previous warning. The critique of Miss Steinem's efforts has, up until now, been a lesson in perseverance in the hope of finding the real Gloria and something of substance. Finding nothing of substance, the sheer boredom of reviewing my notes on this dribble has taken its toll, having thus far covered only 30% of her book.

What completed my nausea at this point was the fact that in taking a breather from Gloria, I decided to research Betty Friedan's **"The Feminine Mystique"** in preparation of the next chapter; only to discover that if placed side by side the two minds would be hard pressed to give a good imitation of a single cell microorganism.

Back to Gloria, just in time for her return to Smith for the class of '56 reunion. She criticized a speech by the college president, Kerr, ". . . of course said nothing about man's responsibility for raising children, cleaning bathrooms, or otherwise limiting his career, as women have traditionally done **when there isn't enough money for household help**."

There will be times when I sarcastically comment briefly just to maintain my sanity completing this mess. Such is the case on page 133, "Like women alcoholics who drink in their own kitchens while costly programs are constructed for executives who drink, or like homemakers subdued with tranquilizers while male patients get therapy and personal attention."

It reminds me of all the wealthy FEMINIST widows who receive the ultimate of care from their dead husbands' estates; while old male winos scrounge the gutters of the Big Apple.

Steinem childishly demeans the father she obviously couldn't tolerate because he apparently wasn't glamorous. She describes her mother's abortive extra-marital affair on page 137, ". . . falling in love with a co-worker at the newspaper who frightened her by being more sexually attractive, more supportive of her work than my father, and finally, nearly bleeding to death with a **miscarriage**."

On her own minor affair immortalized on page 144, Gloria displays her self-discipline and staying power, "I fell out of love when he confessed that he wished I wouldn't smoke or swear . . ."

Being schooled in literacy, not intelligence, Gloria doubles up on her explanations, ". . .women of color, white women . . ."

On the importance of work, she pontificates, "It's just that we are now more likely than ever before to leave our poorly rewarded, low security, high risk job of homemaking . . . more secure, independent, and better paid jobs out of the home."

Yet on page 167, she refers to the year 1979, "Women are 41% of the labor force. 43% are single, widowed, separated or divorced. Women work because we have to . . ." Wait a minute Gloria; it was you who just said the work force was the place to be, compared with the home. Are you suggesting that women join the army or what?

Gloria continuously makes off the wall comments such as:

". . . early consciousness, the problem is that this culturally different form has remained an almost totally female event."

What the girls are really interested in, ". . . radical act of seizing power . . ." Gloria tape recorded some women's rap sessions and concluded women don't talk as much as men. Then goes on to say that women make a contribution to dialog and men give answers and a mini-speech.

Gloria was very excited about a stunningly brilliant comment Germaine Greer quipped to David Susskind on his show one evening, ". . . tell me David, can you tell if I'm menstruating right now or not?" What a show stopper, to which David, too much the gentleman, should have replied, "Take off your panties and let's see, otherwise it's the same as having a bag over your head and asking me if you're throwing up!"

Gloria inadvertently on page 186 again reveals which sex is the devious one; "Women change the register and language around men."

Steinem waxes on about the politics of food in Africa and Asia. She comments that there are strict taboos on the most valued resources of red meat, milk, and some vegetables and fruit. These foods are forbidden to women.

Let's not tell old GLO that, in reality, red meat and milk can be very detrimental to your health, so the women might be letting the men slowly poison themselves to death. But old GLO'S philosophy is that if the men have it then "I" want it.

Gloria is enraged on behalf of the homemaker; "Facts may persuade us of the need to rebel." Fact, according to Gloria and the United Nations, "Homemakers work harder than any other class of worker: an average of 99.6 hours a week." Now that's 99.6 not 99.5 or perhaps 99.7, right Gloria? No doubt .this is typical American housewife.

She is concerned that young American Women are becoming too conservative. She exhorts them onward with impeccable role models, ". . . women students led the cultural revolution in China and campus demonstrations against the Shah . . ."

Congratulations Gloria, with female troops like that you can probably start World War III all by yourself. Those two achievements go down as spawning two of the bloodiest messes in recent history and, as in Russia, led to reigns of total terror. This girl simply has no shame.

Selflessness or selfishness? On page 214, Steinem comments, "I've yet to be on a campus where most women weren't worrying about some aspect of combining marriage, children, and a career."

A zoologist she ain't, but then old Glo's stock-in-trade is disinformation. So what the hell, on page 220 she reprimands American males, ". . . male lions care for their young." Of course everyone but little Glo knows that it's the lionesses that hunt and kill and bring home the bacon, while the King of the Jungle lays around the house all day, eats bonbons, gets fat and complains about the kids. But why spoil a stupid analogy?

From an "Article" in the late 1970's, "There will be little murders in our bedrooms and little love." So what's new Glo?

She demurely makes a confession about one of her infinite duplicities, laughing at Marilyn Monroe; "If there were jokes made in her name . . . I joined in. I contributed to the laughing . . . proving I was nothing like her." By this time, Steinem was in her late 20's or early 30's, obviously a very mature, typically cosmopolitan New York FEMINIST.

Speaking for her contemporaries as well as herself, "Yes, I was American enough to have show business dreams." and went on to say " . . . girls, if we imagined anything other than marrying a few steps up in the world, always dreamed of show business careers."

After college Gloria actually went into show business and even had an agent in Toledo, TOLEDO! Later when she found out she couldn't act, she threw herself into the world of "ARTICLES" probably after she failed to marry a few steps up according to her self-description. Sometime in between fantasies she joined the actors' studio in New York.

She inadvertently discloses the ultimate truth; why so many FEMINISTS fail their primary responsibility, "I have too many fantasies to be a housewife." To which she should have added, and besides it's more glamorous to be an actress, article writer or leader of the FEMINIST movement.

Remember back when Gloria was raving about women in Africa being deprived, by custom, of meat and milk. Did you perhaps notice that she specifically avoided mentioning black males directly? Yet throughout her "Articles" is a constant bitterness towards white males, in particular white Anglo-Saxons. What Gloria wants is revenge of some indefinable nature.

Some Black males in Africa are very insistent on large families and the performance of tribal rituals replete with the mutilation and purification of female genitals at the time of puberty.

American FEMINISTS take much pleasure in demeaning their men while the lunatic fringe and subcultures blame everything on them. Women, in general, will ultimately suffer the most for adhering to FEMINIST fables, as Gloria continues to spin her web of deceit. "The parallel between women and Negroes is the deepest truth of American life for together they form the unpaid and underpaid labor on which America runs."

This kind of inflammable, racist rhetoric is the lowest common denominator of FEMINIST trash verbiage! It is mass character assassination upon the graves of the millions of European, Oriental immigrant males and other minorities who literally killed themselves to provide the very best for their families under the worst possible conditions. But then, American FEMINISTS love to psychologically castrate the world's best providers. What utter stupidity!

Why is it that throughout her book Steinem always screams about Nazi Germany, never Communist Russia? History has far too long neglected the reality of what actually took place in Germany and Spain between 1917 and 1939. There is a later chapter in this book on that very subject, although it may antagonize large influential segments of the American population.

Gloria is filled with revulsion of the many types of surgery performed on women by white male doctors. It's nice to learn from Gloria that male circumcision is painless, no doubt just like fetus abortions - no pain at all! Let's hear it for little Gloria and the "NOW" girls.

Her Rx fantasies are expressed in such inane expressions as, "The International Revolutionary Feminist Government in Exile" or how about this copout, "Fantasies bolster our psychic strength." This, aging old twit is continuously passing through puberty and taking every idiot in America, who can't think for herself, along for the ride.

Continuing her references to Nazi Germany, she tells us that when Hitler came to power he used the Marxist Communists and in particular Jewish women as scapegoats. According to Gloria, German Marxist Communists and in particular, German Jewish women were the forerunners of today's modern FEMINISTS. Some ad campaign to enlist new members that confession will make!

Gloria's instinct for survival is further served by her poison penmanship as she obliquely attacks those who have a difficult time rationalizing her brand of individual female freedom with communism and abortion, "If you are pro-life and support capital punishment or the arms race, then you are inconsistent." She goes blindly on to eulogize how a great FEMINIST movement took place in Germany between 1894 and 1933.

Strange isn't it that the time frame just about parallels the rise of Communism in Soviet Russia. Of course, it's ridiculous to entertain the possibility that there is any connection between the two. The fact of which has been suppressed by the Big Apple network news media for almost a century!

Women according to Gloria aren't the prolific gamblers that men are because; "In fact, women's total instinct for gambling is satisfied by marriage." Believe me, it only wets their appetites, but once again men should heed the thoughts revealed by her cunning little mind, as Gloria begins to warm to her subject matter.

In the 1950's, she brags that Smith girls took their fiancées projects and thesis material to their favorite professors to get a line on the poor guy's value and capabilities. Smith girls then had their professors review the work and answer the question, "Is this guy any good?" This demonstrated ultimate reliance of the pea brain college FEMINIST on her love fantasy, the college professor.

Here is a quote by old Glo that we can all appreciate. Although she doesn't come right out and admit the whole truth, on page 333, " . . . of course, we're now discovering from Freud's letters that he knew such women patients were telling the truth, but went right on blaming the victim in order to make his case histories acceptable to society."

Gloria, the correct interpretation of those revelations is that Sigmund Freud was a liar. As the father of psychiatry, sexually frustrated old Sigmund spawned an entire industry. Along came Jung, Pavlov and Skinner with equally nutty, lopsided conjectures in order to thrive on the gullibility of the general population.

Steinem should change some of her mouthy comments, such as: ". . . <u>if men could menstruate</u>"; to <u>Women dying on the battlefields by the tens of thousands, far from the safety of their homes.</u> On Bella Abzug being courageous, according to Gloria any "NOW" girl crossing the street should receive the Medal of Honor.

Narcissistic dribble exudes from her lips, "If even the work we are doing now were paid according to its <u>logical</u>, comparable value in 'men's worth' we would cause a major redistribution of wealth."

As proof of this major redistribution of wealth Glo offers two beauts; telephone operators in the city hall of New York got $170 per week while precinct police men doing the same job got $306 a week. Little Glo omitted the fact that the policemen are also called upon to function as police officers in the field. Maintenance men, she laments, receive $185 versus cleaning women, who received $170 a week.

Yes Gloria, an obvious total redistribution of wealth! Let's not forget some female newscaster earning $1,000,000 a year interviewing another hard line, complaining FEMINIST while a Marine gives his life for her right to do so. The marine's widow gets some insurance and he gets buried, while people like Gloria Steinem run on at the mouth without any shame, leaving, in their sickly wake, broken homes, broken women and millions of dead fetuses.

III. HERE'S BETTY!

Numbed by the crazy, inane, mumbo jumbo of Gloria Steinem, her trials, lost childhood, utter selfishness and petty grievances, we can "NOW" look forward to meeting the head honcho, Betty Friedan, through her masterpiece, "**The Feminine Mystique**".

For me, it became a duel punishment that no one person should voluntarily undertake. As the brain power trust of the sick preoccupation of 20th century American FEMINISTS with themselves, Steinem and Friedan offer, in their own words, nothing. I mean nothing, absolutely nothing! Just what is it American FEMINISTS crusade for in their selfish search for fulfillment?

Germaine's book was written on false premises, but a thesis developed by an interesting mind. But these other two leaders? Hell, they need help crossing the street! Steinem is a whining nitpicker. Friedan, the great pretender to knowledge, has an absolutely bankrupt mentality. How, after reading her book, anyone could arrive at any other conclusion is beyond imagination.

Having just subjected the reader to Gloria; be forewarned that Betty is equally without material substance. It has occurred to me that those schooled in the rudiments of liberal arts and educational curriculums easily confuse rhetoric with thoughtful substance.

The media necessarily caters to building the reputations of the Steinems and Friedans of this world because by comparison they enhance the relative intelligence of media talking heads to Platonic heights.

Friedan and her darlings seem to take inordinate pride in the dubious distinction that Betty was a psych major at Smith College. Please, if you are ever tempted to value an individual's opinion based on education, money, or titles recall to mind the following first hand encounter I had with a young psych major, at least twenty years after old Betty was similarly knighted at Smith:

Many years ago, I encountered a male, third year psych major attending a large university (which shall remain nameless for obvious reasons), He was sitting beside me on an airplane. Being, at that time, very much interested in early childhood education, I was curious to learn what was taught concerning children's cognitive powers by institutions of higher education.

I inquired of the psyche major as to the abilities of children under the age of five, to reason mathematically. He responded that he had been taught that a youngster's attention span and comprehension were so insignificant at that early an age that simple addition and subtraction were almost beyond their grasp.

When further requested to expound on his knowledge of the length of the attention span of a five-year-old child, he, without hesitation said, "**less than 30 seconds**!" The young psych major's command of the English language and ability to express his opinions were academically impressive, his intellectual quotient, however, bordered on the imbecilic.

You see, at the time, having no education in psychology, I, like other similar fathers, had a young child, a four-year-old son. It just so happened that my son was interested in model ships.

On one occasion, he easily assembled a ship model of over a hundred pieces in about an hour and a half; alone in a room without so much as leaving his pleasurable efforts for a drink of water.

Keeping in mind the example of a psych's level of intelligence, you can now test your boredom quotient by following along with me into the frivolous jungle of the FEMINIST psychology queen.

Feel free at anytime to abandon this chapter and go on the Chapter IV. Hopefully, not before you have learned to fully appreciate ignorance and selfishness.

Betty discloses the secret, unasked question lurking in the brilliant minds of Smith graduates turned suburban housewives, "Is this all?" These women, cites Friedan, "They were taught to pity the neurotic, unfeminine, unhappy women who wanted to be poets or physicists or presidents."

Running as fast as her devious FEMINIST mind can bear the burden, she negatively begs the question, "Who are those that taught her and her sisters this, I have no idea." The hell you don't sweetheart, but then the answer might not fit your fabricated scenario.

Statistics are voluminously cited that continuously return to haunt her erroneous conclusions. Friedan goes on a junkie statistician's rampage of complete disinformation. **<u>Fourteen million girls engaged by 17</u>**! Mind you not pregnant, unmarried and aborting their children like current day FEMINISTS. Just engaged!

Proportion of women's college attendance dropped significantly between 1920 and 1958. Women having fought for higher education now went to college to find a husband. 60% dropped out to marry. **Girls <u>went steady</u> at <u>twelve</u> and <u>thirteen</u>!** Not having sex and getting pregnant and having abortions like today's twelve and thirteen year olds. Just going steady!

The FACTS of her survey are forcefully and dramatically presented, "Where once they had two children, now they had four, five, and six." The verification of her indignation, "In a New York hospital, a woman had a nervous breakdown when she found she could not breast feed her baby."

Imagine if, a single, career minded, free love feminist with similar credentials as Friedan's, had not been successful in maintaining the affection of her lover, and had murdered him! Then the obvious statistical conclusion would be that feminists, brilliant as they are, murder on provocation of lost love. It seems perfectly logical to me. What do you think? Will it fly with Friedanlike logic?

Remember this one. Old Betty just pulls them out of the hat like rabbits. In a few pages later <u>she will completely contradict herself</u>! "Many women no longer left their homes, except to shop (I love that one), chauffeur their children, or attend a social function with their husbands."

Because of this, according to Friedan, enormous shortages occur in vital professions, nursing, social work (my favorite), teaching and you name it.

Where did Betty get all this DATA? The basis for her conjectures come from bias surveys of the typical American girl, a Smith college FEMINIST graduate, representing the upper 1% of American income families.

Somehow, by linking all these patch work numbers, Betty blames the pitiful plight of the Smith girls, the most brilliantly educated women in the world, on seduction by Madison Avenue advertising executives. And who, cites old Betty, is responsible for the preoccupation of these spoiled FEMINISTS' selfish indulgence and mental anguish? You guessed it, the poor bastard that she conned into marrying her.

Let's not chauvinistically surmise for even a single, fleeting minute that one might believe that the blame lay with the unhealthy mental attitude and fantasy world of the Smith FEMINISTS, themselves.

Friedan's meticulously, scientifically designed studies were confined to the most pampered, privileged, selfish group of women to ever grace the face of this planet, the liberal eastern establishment, upper class, FEMINIST, asphalt jungle scavengers of Smith!

Picture if you can, 10,000 Smith graduates, the hardest working women in the world, each with five children, slaving away; giving order after order to their maids, repair men and milkmen. What did old Gloria say, "those housewives that toil 99.6 hours a week."?

All that skill, genius and dedication devoted to the betterment of mankind. Makes you want to cry with unabated anticipation, doesn't it? And just think if Betty had three kids, and Gloria and Harris had none, then some poor Smith FEMINIST has one hell of a lot of kids!

Rather strange statistics for a generation of Smith FEMINISTS who were the most birth control and abortion minded females in America.

It makes you wonder and marvel at Betty's "Statistics" of four, five and six children per Smithy family. More peculiar, is the fact that nowhere in all the Department of Labor and Commerce figures concerning family formations since the beginning of the country can be found an average birthrate of even three children per family.

The things you can learn from Betty - WOW - the enrollment at Smith should skyrocket.

Friedan's fantasies are filled with sympathetic, dashing psychology professors and brilliant Smith FEMINISTS being terrorized by filthy, dirty old, white Anglo-Saxon men of Madison Avenue. Surely it was this group of white male subversives that drove bored FEMINISTS to psychiatrists couches, forced them into unprecedented leisure time, educated them in selfishness, taught them the inability to stand being alone and deprived them of the will power for creative activities.

Oh, how terrible it must be for those poor, tortured, marvelous FEMINISTS of Smith and her sick sister institutions.

Betty bravely brings to the attention of all women, through her book, the poor suffering plight and commiserations of her fellow Smithies, the little dears. "Once she wrote a paper on the graveyard poets; now she writes notes to the milkman."

"Once she determined the boiling point of sulfuric acid; now she determines her boiling point with the overdue repairman . . . the housewife is often reduced to screams and tears."

Stop Betty, please stop, we can't stand the pain, the anguish, the suffering! No silly, not the Smithy housewives, the poor repairmen and milkmen who have to put up with these dumb broads so they can feed their own wives and kids. No sweetheart! You wouldn't understand their women, too real, too tested by the pain of caring.

Had the rotten white Anglo-Saxon male not come along, think of the joy, the happiness. There sits Gloria joyously writing sonnets to Robert Browning while milking cows at five in the morning. And Betty, dear old Betty is washing out her own clothes on the washboard while determining the boiling point of water, by the amount of flesh remaining on her hands in the hot water.

Wait a minute, no so called white Anglo-Saxons? Then perhaps, there would have been no Robert Browning? Okay Gloria, dedicate your sonnets to Fidel Castro.

Better yet, Betty can deliver the milk on time and Gloria can repair the stopped up sewer. Meanwhile the milkman and the repairman can write an entertaining book on the silly Smithies they met. Becoming authors will fulfill the milkman and the repairman's desire for artistic and creative expression so they will not have to ask themselves on their deathbeds, "Is this all?"

Friedan calls the Smith yearning, "The problem without a name." Slowly they gathered together, "They began, hesitantly to talk about it. Later, after they had picked up their children at nursery school and taken them home to nap, two of the women cried, in sheer relief, just to know they are not alone."

Here, once again, we learn of the women valiantly described earlier by Gloria Steinem, ". . . the women who dare to go beyond the frontiers of human existence."

Remember old foot in the mouth Betty? Several pages back she waxed sadly about women no longer leaving their homes, except for shopping, chauffeuring the kids and picking up his majesty. Forgetting that all the girls are cooped up in their homes, she now makes an opposite argument for more sympathy.

"I heard echoes of the problem in college dormitories and semi-private maternity wards, at PTA meetings and luncheons of the League of Women Voters, at suburban cocktail parties, in station wagons waiting for trains, and in snatches of conversations overheard at Schrafft's." **Schrafft's!**

"The groping words <u>overheard</u> from other women, on quiet afternoons when children were at school or **on quiet evenings when husbands worked late.**"

Hardly the description of 99.6 hour work weeks and emotionally crippled shut-ins. Hey gang, what say we all take the afternoon off, belt a few at Schrafft's and eavesdrop on other people's conversations. Let's hurry; cocktails at eight and we don't want to be late! The gathering of these FEMINIST vultures makes the ones in the desert seem charming by comparison.

My goodness, their own little red station wagons, how terrifying Betty. A national catastrophe of monstrous proportions. Who enslaved you in this hideous manner? White Anglo-Saxon males you say. Gee whiz! Imagine that!

And on the sheer genius required of all Smith graduates, measuring the boiling point of sulfuric acid, should you ever be inclined towards intellectual greatness:

1. Very carefully pour into a non-corrosive pot
2. Place pot over well ventilated, high temperature burner
3. Put thermometer in pot
4. Raise temperature slowly
5. Read thermometer when acid begins to boil

Note: Wear rubber gloves so as not to burn your fingers.

With highly intelligent FEMINISTS, variations to these procedures may be permitted, once the student learns to read. These whining, spoiled rotten, childish FEMINISTS should learn how to properly maintain appliances, drive in blinding blizzards and repair washing machines, to say nothing of opening doors and changing tires in order to get their Liberal Arts Degrees.

Betty's literary contribution to double-talk rambles on endlessly. On Page 25 of her book, "All admit to being deeply frustrated at times by the lack of privacy, the physical burden, the routine of family life, the confinement of it."

By a wave of her magic crying towel, Friedan has done away with the Smith girls' nine room houses, lunches at Schrafft's, the quiet evenings when the old man is at the office, the peaceful afternoons when the kids are at school, and when she is alone with her little red station wagon. Or was it the peaceful evenings and quiet afternoons, If Betty so easily forgets, why can't we?

The modern era FEMINIST movement initiated by Friedan's brilliant intellectual effort has been in full swing for some fifty plus years. The results are positively astounding! FEMINISTS join clubs, change jobs (seeking more meaningful work), flood the bars looking desperately for husbands, fill shrink couches by the millions and buy, buy, buy, everything that isn't nailed down.

The Smith FEMINISTS now have their eyes on the ball, but who is responsible for the runaway locomotive? The major culprit inadvertently acknowledges guilt on page 26, "For human suffering there is a reason; perhaps the reason has not been found because the right questions have not been asked, or pressed far enough."

Friedan is master of the monumental understatement while rambling on endlessly. In today's intellectual, college FEMINIST school circles, verboseness, as a shelter for ignorance, is mandatory! She pathetically grinds out 408 pages of useless complaints. Complaints that could have been summarized in a single paragraph.

My name is Betty Friedan. I majored in psychology at Smith. I am very bright. See me write a book. I love my career. Through a very objective survey of my peers, a rotten spoiled gaggle of princess mentality type FEMINISTS, I discovered that we have little to occupy our time and therefore whine and complain about our boredom.

Think of all the printed pages that could have remained trees.

Betty's solution to the problem with no name, caused by white, Anglo-Saxon, Madison Avenue men, is to create a world in which, through government subsidy, every woman is a doctor, lawyer, Supreme Court Justice, president or in a real pinch at least an Indian chief! All contributions toward this ennobling quest gratefully accepted by "NOW" or is it, BUY now?

Her tatterings are filled with frightening stories of women trapped in squirrel cage homes. About women who have sexually starved hungers. FEMINISTS, who are plagued by strange new problems brought on by housewife fatigue; not to be confused with office fatigue brought about by working for a living. She goes on to say, "Housewives are addicted to tranquilizers."

Intelligent, career minded FEMINISTS wouldn't do that. At least not before puffing a joint, just for recreational purposes mind you, sniffing a little coke, just to take the edge off and taking prescription anti-depressant drugs. Of course Betty, we understand.

To our great relief, Betty found many clues. She tells us what led her to the truth. The white, Anglo-Saxon male, was the evil that preyed on American Women. It lurked in large families, character pathologies, and sexual problems.

Undauntedly, Betty and the Smithies met the challenge of those monstrous evils head-on. Thanks to their unstinting efforts and self-sacrifice, we are now blessed with the fruits of their labor.

MORE THAN EVER COMPLETELY DYSFUNCTIONAL
FAMILIES
EVER GROWING POPULATION OF POOR WHITE
WOMEN
ONE MILLION ABORTIONS EVERY YEAR
SKY HIGH BIRTH RATES BY UNMARRIED WOMEN
CREATIVE NEW NEUROSES
HERPES
AIDS
AND OH, YES! SEXUAL PROBLEMS

Thanks Betty, thanks Smithies, because of you, today the world in which we live is a better place. We all feel much more secure, self-fulfilled and loved.

On the needs of her FEMINIST followers and herself, Betty's discloses their level of greediness in an almost unbelievable narcissism wrapped in a plea for understanding by one or more of her interviewees. On page 32, **"I want something more than my husband and my children and my home."** Those unrelenting egocentric words, despite Friedan's sympathetic surrounding rhetoric, lay naked the utter GREED, greed beyond redemption that fills the bones to the very marrow of these parasites. The key words are, SOMETHING MORE, not in place of, but more and More and **MORE**!

Coupled with Gloria's 220 "I"s in 18 pages and Betty's constant rephrasing of relentless selfishness disguised as freedom, American FEMINISTS and like minded males nod their heads in some form of childish agreement depending on which fantasies fulfill their emotional needs on an instantaneous basis.

American FEMINISTS today have about as much good sense regarding the advice of Steinem and Friedan as women had in

30

adhering to the pronouncements of Queen Victoria. All these opposite and emotional cravings are the result of slavish adherence of women to the ill-conceived theories of other women, not men.

Betty tells us that great accomplishments were being carried out throughout the world while American Women were in desperate straits. To prove her point, she extols the virtues of Castro's Cuba and the formation of the New African States. Fifty years have passed since Betty's first pronouncements of her FEMINIST logic. Most people in the African States are starving to death and the Russians, who themselves are now broke, had for years pumped millions of dollars a day, every day, into Castro's economy, which has now completely failed.

Cuba became a Communist showpiece of free medical care and education for all, paid for by enslaving young Cuban men as surrogate cannon fodder for Russian imperial ambitions in Africa. All of these Friedan "success stories" were total failures. Undoubtedly, in her warped view of world events, anything is successful when not involving white Anglo-Saxon bogie men.

Friedan's ideal, revolutionary FEMINIST was born of pulp literature in the 1930's that she gloriously describes on page 38. "They were New Women, creating with a gay determined spirit a new identity for a life of their own . . . the major heroines . . . were career women - happily, proudly, adventurously, attractive career women who loved, and were loved by men . . . there was a definite aura that their individuality was to be admired . . . these heroines were usually marching towards some goal or vision of their own. Struggling with some problem of work. . . . when they found their man . . . the heroine of one of these stories met and fell in love at an ad agency where they both worked . . . but the moral, in 1939, was that if she kept her commitment to herself, she did not lose the man, if he was the right man."

An Ad agency!?

Don't go away folks. I am not making this up. It's all in Betty's book. She moves right along on pages 40-41, "The next morning Sarah solos, Henry stepped away, slamming the cabin door shut, and swung the ship about for her, she was alone, there was a heady moment when everything she has learned left her . . . Henry's girl! She smiled. No, she wasn't Henry's girl. She was Sarah."

Here we have Betty Friedan's ultimate FEMINIST, Sarah! Sarah, beautiful Sarah, Our heroine role model, Sarah, who was taught by Henry to fly, in Henry's airplane, using Henry's gasoline, all paid for by Henry's money, the dirty rotten, white Anglo-Saxon, capitalist pig!

Good old cuckolded Henry who helped the brave, independent Sarah into the airplane, closed the door for the strong, brave Sarah, and turned the airplane around so that bright, beautiful, young Sarah would not take off in the wrong direction and kill herself!

Seriously these are the kinds of FEMINIST quacks that want to be your intrepid leaders in a Cuban style revolution to free the world from the domination of the white Anglo-Saxon male, who was born, bred and raised by . . . no, not a Chinese lady . . . no, not an African woman . . . Serbian? I wonder who the hell is responsible for this guy anyway?

Only forty some pages of Betty have been read and she is just warming up. We have been treated to just a peek at the brilliant mind of "NOW". Come on give me a break, admit it, I'm the only one who has read even one of these stupid books let alone all three.

No one could have taken these nitwits seriously. I know. It was the parades. Everybody loves a parade. It was the parades that made you a FEMINIST; wasn't it? Come on, we're all dying to know? You didn't do it because you actually read their books? Nobody could be that dumb!

Friedan goes on to speak of weekly allowances, and charge accounts . . . ah yes, the need for a revolutionary to have her own charge account. Then there is Ed, some guy who after working all day doesn't like coming home and dusting the furniture and vacuuming while his distressed, neurotic FEMINIST wife has been visiting with Betty all day at Schrafft's.

It seems Ed's wife doesn't appreciate being a combat soldier, changing the oil in her station wagon or cleaning out sewers, but she would be terrific at flying Henry's airplane.

Betty quotes one of her editors. The editor realizes the problem at last, "We suddenly realized that all these women at home with their three and a half children were miserably unhappy."

Hell, any American husband married to a FEMINIST could have told you that in thirty seconds after the poor bastard got married. And then there are those mythical three and a half kids Betty refers to when she comes down off her FEMINIST high of four, five and six. Believe me ladies that last 1/2 kid is hell to raise. Little bugger gets into everything!

If, as Betty assures us, the Smith FEMINISTS represent the best and brightest, it confirms the fact that the old time hillbilly men were absolutely correct; for God's sake, keep'em barefoot and down on the farm, where they can do no harm!

Twenty pages further into this mess, Betty still wants her own airplane and on page 71 describes the desperate plight of an enslaved Smithy, WHO MARRIED A DOCTOR. "I never thought it through until I was thirty-six, and my husband was so busy with his practice that he couldn't **entertain me every night**."

You guessed it. Her husband was busy patiently listening to other FEMINISTS bend his sympathetic ear all day long about their mistreatment at the hands of their own husbands, while falling madly in love with their understanding doctor.

Those other FEMINISTS would die for the chance to marry her doctor husband and live with him happily ever after, well at least until after the wedding. A bright Smithy by all accounts, it took her only thirty-six years to figure out what she wanted. **<u>Entertainment every night!</u>** Yep, she is definitely a "NOW" girl!

One of Gloria's great lines was apparently inspired by this FEMINIST quote in Betty's book; "The feminists were pioneering on the front edge of women's evolution." Betty then riles at the enslavement of American women by talking about men taking their pleasure with women, the fact that women are not allowed to become fully human, and the unfair covenants in the marriage vows of the Christian religions.

Betty complains that God's most precious material, women, **is entirely wasted in the role of mothers and wives.**

Other early, women revolutionaries, Betty tells us, didn't like to parade around in bloomers, because, are you ready for this one, because only pretty Mrs. Bloomer looked good in them. Then there was Susan Anthony. She became a rabid FEMINIST, not because of the evils of men, but because her beautiful mother and sister made fun of her crossed eyes! Later in life she felt betrayed by her fellow FEMINISTS. They began to marry and have babies. Boy, how history repeats itself.

Betty loves the brutality of one old English FEMINIST, Ida Ross Wylie; who took great pleasure in knocking some guy into the orchestra pit at a FEMINIST rally.

Friedan, the eminent psychologist, lectures us on the greatness of Sigmund Freud, "The Feminine Mystique derives its power from Freudian thought; . . . because the very nature of Freudian thought makes it virtually invulnerable to question."

Betty then goes on to say, "I know that Freud's discovery of the unconscious workings of the mind was one of the great breakthroughs in man's pursuit of knowledge, she knows that the science built in that discovery has helped many suffering men and women."

Her piece de resistance:

"No one can question the basic genius of Freud's discoveries or the contribution he has made to our culture, nor do I question the effectiveness of psychoanalysis as it is practiced today by **Freudian and anti-Freudian."**

It would require a more Christian-like soul then my own to refrain from commenting on Betty's Godlike blessing upon another twentieth century nut and Betty's own self-contradictory statements.

Sigmund Freud was a neurotic, poor tortured soul, who attempted to inflict and justify his psychotic illness on his patients and those closest to him. Sexually inhibited, he was ever the voyeur. His patients lay upon a couch because he could not bear to face them. Freud's gift to Western civilization was not the miracle of psychoanalysis but the addiction of cocaine.

No lack of knowledge or experience hindered Betty's following declaration, "relativity, which in recent years has changed our whole approach to scientific knowledge, is harder, and therefore easier to understand than the social scientist's relativity."

Betty, we wait with baited breath while you explain the theory of relativity. In the cases of both you and Gloria, the age-old adage once again proves infallible. A little knowledge is a very dangerous thing.

Friedan comments that some social theorists (a great group of know-it-alls) suspect that the dying Austrian Empire caused the sexual preoccupation of Sigmund Freud's patients. FREUD'S PATIENTS preoccupation with sex?! You mean Sigmund's preoccupation, don't you? The old guy positively drooled over the subjects of penis envy, Oedipus complex, the autocratic authority of the father (his own), his own fantasies of sexual jealousy of his father and sexual love of his mother, a regular Charley Manson.

His genius mentality can best be seen from Betty's description of Freud's understanding of early child development, ". . . the child gets his sexual pleasure first by mouth, from the mother's breast, then from his bowel movements. These are now seen as stages of human growth . . . "

Gloria tells us that housewives kill themselves, working 99.6 hours a week then Betty quotes some social scientist to prove just the opposite, ". . . the housewife role has declined to the point where it scarcely approaches a full time occupation for a vigorous person."

Kind of makes you wonder doesn't it? A "functional theoretician of sociology" is the foot-in-mouth, oversized vocabulary Friedan uses to describe one who takes relatively simple courses in college and comes up with harebrained ideas later on in life.

Margaret Mead, at the time, was a living legend to old Betty. Friedan informs us that Mead's work had a profound effect on the FEMINISTS of Betty's generation. She was a true symbol of the woman thinker in America; studied by FEMINISTS taking courses in anthropology, sociology, psychology, education, marriage and family life.

Betty goes on to say Margaret was revered by one and all, especially FEMINIST pediatricians, psychiatrists and by progressive young male seminarians. And she is read over and over again in women's magazines. Betty's vision of the future in Communist America is clearly based on the teachings of Old Margaret.

Margaret Mead's musings made a great many American FEMINISTS envy the serene SENSUOUSNESS of bare breasted Samoan women, fantasizing themselves as languorous savages, breasts unfettered by civilization's brassieres, and brains undisturbed by pallid, manmade knowledge or the goals of civilization.

Nakedness in Samoa is idealistically wonderful, but New York City in a snow storm? Come on Betty, really. Margaret loved the way the natives screwed, but she wasn't too crazy about kids. Off with the man-made contraption of a brassiere, in with the IUD, another man-made device.

Betty forgot to tell you that all those gorgeous Samoans are seventeen years and younger. WOW! Have you seen what happens after that! Speaking of Margaret, Betty had this to say, "She has moved on the frontiers of thought and added to the super structure of our knowledge." Sounds very much like the Titanic to me.

You see, Margaret was not only extremely bias in her opinions but her fantasy anthropology ramblings have been refuted by no less than the Samoan people themselves. Margaret's visits were brief, idyllic and highly romanticized. Her idyllic accounts are filled with tons of rhetoric. There was no substance to her writings. They were based almost entirely on the fantasies of teenage native girls. She was not allowed to partake of adult activities or permitted to really associate with the adults.

Friedan takes a couple of free pokes at her fellow sisters and finds the old days better, ". . . after class, arguing about what the professor said - Economic Theory, Political Philosophy, the History of Western Civilization, Sociology 21, Science and Imagination, even Chaucer."

Good Lord Betty, those are garbage courses, helping to create the illusion that one is being let into a secret world of intellectual stimulation. My nine-year-old son enjoyed reading Chaucer, as did many other grade school and high school students

Another of Friedan pithy remarks, ". . . education of femininity also spread from Mills, Stephens, and the finishing schools (where its basis was more traditional than theoretical) to the proudest bastions of the women's Ivy League, the colleges which pioneered higher education for women in America, and were noted for their uncompromising intellectual standards."

My sincere apologies go to the Stephen's women. Friedan has no taste. Uncompromising intellectual standards . . . pat me on the back everybody. Betty lets us know, she is an intellectual and a Smith graduate. Well, la de da for you Betty. Would love to see an intellectual shoot-out between you and those "feminine" Midwestern girls from Stephen's, who some of us ignoramuses thought were special, very bright women.

". . . by never achieving the hard core of self that comes not from fantasy but from mastering reality, these girls are doomed to suffer ultimately . . ."

But Betty, that's exactly what I have been trying to tell you about yourself. However, you do it so much better and subconsciously at that. Friedan chastises the American Women, who lived through the Second World War, for rushing the returning G.I.'s into marriage, "It has not happened in other countries . . . women did not run in panic."

I know this is a difficult concept for Betty to grasp, women in places such as Dresden, London and Hiroshima had no homes to which they could return in panic, much less live and marry healthy, whole young men. Those no good white American Anglo-Saxon men again, won the war and saved her little ass.

Those feminine American Women, you mean the ones that drove the fork lift trucks, riveted the airplanes, worked the assembly lines and raised the kids? Not so surprising, they found no great intellectual satisfaction in hard physical labor. After the war, home and family and husband looked mighty good to them, as it did to the boys who came back in one piece.

Of course, those women didn't know about the millions and millions of career opportunities to become a doctor, lawyer, etc., and neither did their sweethearts, the returning G.I.'s who went back to the coal mines and the steel mills.

Women, American Women, after the second World War were, according to Betty Friedan, quitters, "Women went home again just as men shrugged off the bomb, forgot the concentration camps, condoned corruption, and fell into helpless conformity; just as thinkers avoided the complex larger problems of the postwar world." Where, one wonders, was Betty?

We know! Betty Friedan was on the lawn of Smith College reading Chaucer!

Never in the history of two centuries of the " FEMINIST" movement for EQUAL RIGHTS, not in the war of 1812, the Civil War, the Spanish American War, World War I, the great World War II, the Korean War, and certainly not the Vietnam War was there been a single organized protest by American FEMINISTS for the right to be drafted.

Not one FEMINIST in two hundred years has picketed her Senator, the Pentagon, appeared on a talk show, wrote an article, or gave a single speech about their right to be drafted at age eighteen.

Equal rights at the height of the FEMINISTS revolution was not meant by FEMINISTS to grant them the right to die next to a white Anglo-Saxon young man, a Jewish boy, a young black man or any other American male.

America, you see is populated by a special breed of whining, selfish FEMINISTS who constantly bitch and scream more, More, MORE. Even other women "NOW" see them for what they really are; "The Grass is always greener for the FEMINISTS of Smith!"

If Nazi Germany was terrible and the Russians so heroic, why weren't the FEMINISTS lining up in droves to fight in Europe as volunteers, or at least as mercenaries? If Jane Fonda is so convinced that America was the great evil in Vietnam, why didn't she volunteer to fight for the North Vietnamese?

Is everyone finally getting the point? These brave FEMINISTS are two bit phonies from the tips of their toes to the last hair on their empty, greedy heads. Wouldn't that have been a heart grabber to see Gloria in her diapers and Friedan in helmet and fatigues slugging it out with the Germans, side by side with their brave Russian comrades on the Eastern front. Better still, Aerobic Jane, slithering down the Ho Chi Min trail, one bug infested evening!

Friedan's love of Communist Russia spills over as she quotes from Dr. Spock (who later apologized for his earlier misconceptions regarding early childhood development).

"Russian children, whose mothers usually have some purpose in their lives besides motherhood, - they work in medicine, science, education, industry, government, art - seem somehow more stable, adjusted, mature, than American children, whose full time mothers do nothing but worry about them. Could it be that Russian women are somehow better mothers because they have a serious purpose in their lives?"

Spock's _expert_ sociology opinion can be relied upon by the FEMINISTS of Smith to reinforce their intellectually impressed education that Communist Russia, for fantasized, revolutionary, romantic reasons is a model political ideology to be revered by one and all. Uneducated people aren't privileged to learn from romantic literature and the teachings of social scientists such intellectual, secret knowledge.

Less "brilliantly" educated Americans ignorantly believe that a nation of people founded on Marxist-Lenin principles is to be pitied not emulated. Such a ridiculous conclusion is based upon common sense, not romantic fantasies, such as:

- A Government that murdered millions of its own people.
- A nation ruled for almost thirty years by a certified maniac, not Adolph Hitler, Joseph Stalin!
- A nation which builds a wall, not to keep people out, but to keep them in captivity.
- A nation admittedly the alcoholic capitol of the world.

But then what does the average common sense American know? After all, Smith College has all the books and social scientists. Yes siree! Smith has real social scientists and psychology majors. You should see 'em, real honest to God psychology majors!

These marvelous geniuses know from reading Dr. Spock that in Russia there is a wonderful land of liberated women with millions and millions, or as Carl Sagan might respond, Billions and Billions, of female doctors, scientists, teachers, industry leaders, governmental department heads, artists and writers. And you know what, they only have one or two token women sweeping streets, shucking corn and cleaning sewers.

Smith FEMINISTS, strong in their beliefs, would have flocked to this modern day Shangri-La but they had a higher duty to mankind. They stayed in the evil country of America, suffered outrage and torture in their nine room homes and little red station wagons while enduring frigid cold winters huddling together in a penal institution infamously referred to as Schrafft's.

Suffer as they may, they would stand shoulder to shoulder, left hand across their breasts, right hand held high, as they took an oath to tell the truth, the WHOLE truth and nothing but the truth to save American Women from a fate worse than death.

After the FEMINIST REVOLUTION in America is completed, every top executive position of power will be given to African American women (the girls wouldn't want to start off practicing discrimination). First a black woman will be made President of the United States, and then other black women will be made presidents of all U. S. corporations, then in order of power, senators, legislators, vice presidents, doctors, lawyers, dentists, university administrators and professors.

There will be plenty of "Career" opportunities for the remaining ten million or more of their black sisters and the 100 million remaining other American Women. These remaining 98% of American Women can become assembly line workers, telephone repair girls, salesgirls, lady plumbers, steel mill operators, ditch diggers and garbage collectors. The list of fulfilling career opportunities is mind boggling!

American FEMINISTS can then take revenge on helpless white, Anglo-Saxon men, forcing them to stay home, giving them little blue station wagons, raping them in the evenings, and making them take naps in the afternoon when the six kids are in school.

At night, the men would be forced to go to Schrafft's and complain about their wives. In the dead of winter these poor defenseless males, under guard, would be sent to a health and beauty spas in southern California. How terribly evil and cruel American FEMINISTS can be!

There are terrible inequities in the human created realities of an earthly existence. Women as well as men have created and fostered these inequities in all societies throughout the recorded history of the human race. No doubt such will remain the case for any existence allocated to human beings yet unborn.

While fantasizing about a FEMINIST, Communistic takeover, Friedan throughout her book launches into a tirade on Madison Avenue Advertising. Yet at one time was permitted to see some marketing surveys. At least Betty said she saw such information. From such supposed surveys, Betty, the brilliant Smith FEMINIST, drew some very stupid conclusions:

"Somehow, someone must have figured out that women will buy more things if they are kept in the underused, nameless yearning, energy-to-get-rid-of state of being a housewife."

"It would take a clever economist to figure out what would keep our affluent economy going if the housewife market began to fall off."

". . . the career Woman or would be career Woman was a minority, but an extremely 'unhealthy one' from the sellers' standpoint; advertisers warned that it would be to their advantage not to let this group get any larger."

Friedan goes to great lengths to convince her radical sisters that if housewives go back to work, then "Capitalism" will fail because career FEMINISTS are too bright, too intelligent and too self-sacrificing to buy things and, therefore, the economy of America will collapse.

These silly ideas of Friedan's are not idle, isolated remarks in her book, but major premises of her "FEMINIST" revolutionary dream. The personality conflicts within this confused and rambling individual are again revealed in a quote describing a harried housewife.

"So a **Scarsdale woman fired <u>her maid</u>**, and even doing her own housework and the usual community work, could not use up all her energy."

Friedan and Steinem continue throughout their individual diatribes, to quote authorities and render illogical and contradictory proof statements in order to bolster their psychotic schizophrenia.

For the uninitiated, psychotic schizophrenia is insane mental disassociation. People who are of this nature, such as Sigmund Freud, absolve themselves of their internal conflicts by transferring their own aberrational behavior onto the somewhat orderly society in which they find themselves institutionalized.

That last verbosity of mine has all the makings of a Doctoral Thesis Candidacy in any one of the great liberal universities in the United States. I could also be dead wrong, but who cares?

On the causes of female sexual problems, Betty hypothesizes that if women followed their independent career paths their sexual desires would also be satisfied. To ready us for her brilliant solution to another capitalistic impressed problem, Friedan offers the following examples to prove her conclusions:

"A number of the more disagreeable sexual phenomena of this era can be seen now as the inevitable result of that ludicrous consignment of millions of women to spend their days at work eight year olds could do."

"Shortly after weaning her fifth baby from the breast, at thirty three, she had her first affair. She discovered it gave me the wonderful feeling again, to give my whole self to someone else."

"Sex is the only frontier open to women who have always lived within the confines of the feminine mystique."

"Instead of fulfilling the promise of infinite orgasmistic bliss, sex in America of the feminine mystique is becoming a strangely joyless national compulsion."

"This sexual boredom is betrayed by the ever growing size of the Hollywood starlet's breasts, by the sudden emergence of the male phallus as an advertising gimmick."

". . . the frustrated sexual hunger of American women has increased and their conflicts over femininity have intensified."

"I found evidence of these phenomena everywhere. There is, as I have said an air of exaggerated unreality about sex today . . ."

"But in the past decade there has been an enormous increase in the American preoccupation with sex and sexual fantasy."

"The most striking new sexual phenomena, however, was the increased and evidently 'insatiable' lasciviousness of best-selling novels and periodical fiction, whose audience is primarily women."

". . . become apparent as the image of males lusting after women gave way to the new image of women lusting after males."

"The air of unreality that hovers over my interviews with suburban housewife sex-seekers, the unreality that pervades the sex preoccupied novels, plays, and movies-as it pervades the ritualistic sex talk at suburban parties."

"Is there, after all, a link between what is happening to the women in America and increasingly overt male homosexuality?"

"Psychiatrists have explained that the key problem in promiscuity is usually low self-esteem . . ."

"Compulsive sexual activity, homosexual or heterosexual, usually vales a lack of potency in other spheres of life."

". . . it takes a mature mother with a firm core of self, whose own sexual, instinctual needs are integrated with a social conscience."

Betty Friedan wrote these pathology disorders about the American women of the 1950's! She attributes the causes to women being housewives.

She claimed it was sexual dysfunctional proof of the failure of the American Woman's "Feminine Mystique" of housewifeliness. Go back now and read the list of sexual fantasy preoccupations of women in the 1950's. Sound familiar?

Of course they do. Every one of those examples of feminine sexual dysfunction is ten times worse today in the era of the "Career FEMINIST ". FEMINISTS have been engaged in the "NOW" movement far longer, since the early 1960's than the women after World War II were engaged in just being housewives. By Friedan-like logic, applying her arguments to "NOW" and ERA, both are massively greater failures than the "Feminine Mystique".

The third fraudulent cornerstone of this gal's grand hypothesis is the **escalation of violence in America <u>in the 1950's</u>!**

"And there were ominous signs across the nation of mounting uncontrollable violence among young parents and their children trapped in passive dependence."

"It was said, finally, that not the SS but the prisoners themselves became their own worst enemy. Because **they** <u>could not bear to see the situation as it really was</u> . . ."

The first of the above two quotations by Friedan, to validate her premises, actually delineates her own ignorance. Friedan accepts the statement on its face value. Her conclusions by any measurement of comparative results are fallacious! Friedan is her own worst enemy. She simply cannot admit her own ignorance.

"The feminine mystique has succeeded in burying millions of American women alive. There is no way out of <u>their comfortable concentration camps</u> except by finally putting forth an effort . . ."

Betty is not talking about the insane grossness and unheard of domestic violence in America in <u>the Twenty First Century</u>, when all the FEMINISTS are "Career Women" No, no, you don't understand!

Betty Friedan noted psychologist from Smith College, is telling us that **in 1963**! If American Women are not allowed to have careers then by inference we can anticipate domestic violence to increase at epidemic rates. Conversely, if American Women all go back to work, domestic violence will rapidly decline. This gal would be better off as a ghostwriter for Grimm's fairy tales than as a leader of any "movement", including her own.

Preceding her "Final Solution" to the transition of American Women trapped into the Feminine Mystique to American FEMINISTS <u>trapped in the Career Mystique</u>, Betty comically comes to grips with an all too brief moment of truth, page 349:

"There are, of course, a number of **practical problems** involved in making a serious professional commitment."

Just when we thought old Betty had hit on a serious consideration, her quick, incisive, mental faculties recall the perfect solution.

"Over and over, women told me that the crucial step for them was simply to take the first trip to the <u>alumnae employment</u> office."

Whew! For a minute Betty, I thought you might say something idiotic, like, look in the jobs available listings in your local newspapers or now, apply on the internet. Okay, all you American FEMINIST career seekers don't walk; run to your nearest Smith **<u>alumnae employment agency</u>**. Hurry up! This week they're running a special on "Doctor" jobs.

Friedan, near the end of her book, presses home her own "Final Solution". American Women by the millions have been breathlessly waiting for her "secret".

"The key to the trap is, of course, education."

"But I think that education, and only education, has saved, and can continue to save, American Women from the greater dangers of the feminine mystique."

"These 200 Smith graduates have their counterparts in women all over the country, women of intelligence and ability, fighting their way out of the housewife trap, or never really being trapped at all because of their education. But these graduates of 1942 were among the last American women educated before the feminine mystique."

"I would suggest first of all an intensive concentrated re-immersion in, quite simply, the humanities."

"Who knows what women can be when they are finally free to become themselves."

What can I say to those patient, long suffering readers who have stuck with me throughout the three chapter recap of all these silly FEMINIST self-delusions? Friedan predicted and gave completely biased, non-statistical survey evidence to support:

A. American Women would be fulfilled by a "Career".

B. The American economy would collapse when American Women went to work, because of all the stupid conclusions ever reached; they would not buy "THINGS".

C. American Women would no longer be preoccupied

D. with sexual fantasies, romance novels, movies, magazines, etc.

E. Domestic violence was caused because the home was a concentration camp and violence was reaching epidemic proportions in <u>1963</u>!

All of the major premises upon which Betty Friedan built her arguments for an American Women's FEMINIST Revolution were completely and absolutely FALSE, **without a single redeeming accurate conclusion; shot through with half truths, self-contradictory analogies, and falsely applied "statistics".**

It is very important that Americans, especially "Career FEMINISTS", media newscasters, talk show hosts, and those who profit from the "FEMINIST" movement, remember in the years to come how they have contributed to the deep poverty and loneliness that millions of human beings, mostly AMERICAN FEMINISTS, will experience.

Poverty and loneliness are the direct result of the popularization of the nonsensical ideas of irresponsible FEMINISTS such as the Steinems and Friedans of this world.

Those who bask in the glory of their ignorant followers must in the end be held accountable for the net results of their arrogant stupidity. Before we take leave of Betty, Gloria, and Germaine, I'll put forth the following tiny pieces of information to see how it fits the results of the "Careering" of American FEMINISTS as hyped by the "GIRLS". According to data accumulated by the National Center for Health Statistics:

In **1960, 5.3%** of American births were to unmarried women. Despite approximately 1.5 million abortions per year, in **1979, 17.1%** of American births were to unwed mothers. Perhaps we should have dedicated those 365 days as "The Year of the FEMINIST "! Now, in the Twenty-First Century AD those figures are astronomical.

Arrogance, in the presence of overwhelming evidence to the contrary of one's efforts, is the measure of one's ignorance. In the face of all the years of accumulated evidence in contradiction of her theories, when asked in an interview (Detroit News, 1/2/84), "What mistakes has the movement made?" Betty Friedan glibly pronounced, "Not a lot."

"Frustrations, irritations, struggles and distortions are bound to occur in any movement. We can say, "If only we'd gotten ERA passed," or "If there hadn't been a conservative backlash, but there were those things and that's not surprising. I don't find it necessary to cry doom-and-gloom and bemoan the fact that young women take it all for granted."

The woman is absolutely incredible. The reality of the situation is not the opposition to her ideas; but the fact that every one of her pet conclusions, which formed the basis for her ideas, has proven completely false!

In the very same edition of the Detroit News on page one was a summary of the results of the Cuban Revolution, 25 years after its conception.

- Russia was subsidizing Cuba to the tune of 4 billion dollars a year.

- <u>1/2 of Cuba's 10 million population was born after 1958. Meat, rice, sugar, milk, clothing, shoes, appliances and gasoline are rationed.</u>
- <u>A single pair of homemade shoes cost $40.</u>

A summation of the results of the Cuban Revolution was aptly quoted by a retired old mechanic still in Cuba:

"The revolution is marvelous, now we are all poor together."

The plaintive realization of a gray-haired old man in Havana's San Ignacio Street:

"It may be all right for the young people, they don't know anything else. In the old days I was only a poor shoemaker, but at least I could do what I pleased . . . Freedom has no price."

IV. GERMANY AND SPAIN
1917 – 1939

The feminists unashamedly rave about how great Communism is. Betty raves about the opportunities for women in Communist Russia. Steinem tells us very specifically that when Hitler came to power he used the Marxist Communists and especially Jewish women as scapegoats.

According to Gloria, German Marxist Communists and in particular, German Jewish women were the forerunners of today's modern FEMINISTS. So what part did these intellectuals and forerunner FEMINISTS take in spreading worldwide Communism as so enthusiastically endorsed by American FEMINISTS?

This writer is now going to enter forbidden territory. It is the most treacherous ground any Western civilization commentator on the affairs of human beings dares to make public. Some of this subject matter has been obscurely mentioned in previous texts but has never been fully revealed in a book published for popular American readership.

My sincere apologies to the hardworking, loyal, American Jewish population and to those Jews worldwide who have suffered so terribly throughout history because what follows is necessary in order to counter all the spurious arguments Steinem and Friedan use to convince American Women that Communism and specifically FEMINISM are the wave of the future. Also, this chapter is necessary in order to counteract the Communist and Extreme Socialism Indoctrination of all our children in the current Radicalized Public Educational System.

There are powerful vested contrarian interests in this country. They would prefer, either from past embarrassment or from what is yet to be gained by denying the truth, that the American Public remains manipulatively ignorant of these facts.

What the Nazi's did to the Jews, in and prior to the Second World War, was abominable. Beyond civilized comprehension. The same can be said for the elimination of five million peasants by the Russian Communists, the murder of four thousand Polish military officers by the Russian army; the murder of innocent Jewish children by Palestinians, the bombing of Vietnamese children by Americans, the air raids by Jewish pilots that kill Palestinian children and other civilians in retaliation raids, etc. There are not pages enough in the universe to list the atrocities of human beings towards each other.

Jews, the world over, grieve for those murdered in the Nazi Holocaust. They also believe it is just to hold liable Western civilization and in particular most Germans for such heinous crimes.

There are, however, those intrinsic myths in the human psyche that permit intellectual pursuits in defense of one's own objectives in order to escape reality, or to satisfy the fragile guile of a flawed social fabric of belief easing the guilt pangs through participatory duplicity.

Adolph Hitler was a horribly evil, aberrational instrument of torture befalling the everyday Jewish people because of the absolutely, factually documented, Jewish intellectuals' **<u>Communist</u>** attempt to overthrow the failing German Republic.

A Republic which failed due mostly to the greed of the victors of the First World War and the absolutely insane, idiotic pursuit of Jewish intellectuals and equivalent comrades to justify their own existence as Communist revolutionaries.

Had there been no Communist revolutionary threat in post World War I Germany, Adolph Hitler and the Nazi party would have never come to power!

To begin this exploration into the Jewish FEMINISTS and Jewish intellectual propagandists who initiated, the worldwide, Russian Communistic revolution, the origins can be traced back into antiquity and fast-forwarded into the present renewal of Israel as a nation.

ANTIQUITY:

Old Testament quotations from Deuteronomy, one of the five Books of the Jewish Pentateuch

"When the Lord your God brings you into the land you are entering to possess and drives out before you many nations . . . and when the Lord has delivered them over to you and you have defeated them, then destroy totally . . . show them no mercy" 7:1

"However in the cities of the nations the Lord your God is giving you as an inheritance, do not leave alive anything that breathes. Completely destroy them." 20:16

THE PRESENT RENEWAL OF ISRAEL AS A NATION:
Arabs wage religious war, not territorial one, Seymore Heller, Rogers Park.

The Palestinians are the descendants of the Canaanites; the original inhabitants of the land that, since 1948, is called Israel. Throughout the ages the land has been known as Palestine. The ancestors of the Palestinians were in possession of that land some 2,000 years before the arrival of the first ancient Hebrews in 1200 BC. The Palestinians have been continuous residents throughout history under various empires, including Romans, Ottomans, the British and now the nation of Israel.

The ancient Jews reigned in Palestine for only 63 years under the rules of David and Solomon. Only during this brief period was the land called Israel. In order for the Zionist Jews to establish a

"National Home" (promised the Jews in the secret British Balford Agreement for German Zionist support in World War I), a way had to be found to disenfranchise the Palestinians. Thus the Palestinians became expendable.

The reason for the Palestinian exodus from Israel was panic and fear inspired by Jewish terrorism on a scale the Palestinians have never come close to matching. Hundreds of Palestinian men, women and children were murdered in villages of Deir Yassin, Nasr Al-din, Al-Zeitouneh, Al-bina, Albasso and Safsaf in the years following the creation of Israel. Jewish terrorist groups included the Irgun, headed by former Israel Prime Minister Menachem Begin and the Stern Gang headed by former Israeli Prime Minister Yitzhak Shamir

---

STONE-THROWERS SHOULD BE SHOT, SAYS SHAMIR, Associated Press-Jerusalem, Thursday, September 1, 1988.

He called for changing Israel policy and urged that civilians and soldiers to open fire without first firing warning shots.

A painful Stand on Israel, by Woody Allen
(Time magazine)

"I mean, fellas, are you kidding? Beating of people by soldiers to make examples of them? Breaking the hands of men and women so they can't throw stones? Dragging civilians out of their houses at random to smash them with sticks in an effort to terrorize a population into quiet?"

"Am I reading correctly? Were food and medical supplies withheld to make a rebellious community uncomfortable? Were real bullets fired to control crowds and rubber ones only when the United States objected? Are we talking about state-sanctioned brutality and even torture?"

Holocaust museums should be established in every country but also with full disclosure as to Jewish involvement in similar heinous crimes throughout the twentieth century. Such even-handed honesty would be a constant reminder of mankind's inhumanity, and also a reminder that no race, nationality or creed is superior or inferior to any other.

The brief summary of the events and results of Communist activities during the Twentieth Century is that deep dark secret that has been systematically expunged from Western consciousness. Begging the reader's pardon for brevity herein is that historical information.

The historical truth of the Russian Revolution into an institutionalized atheistic State has as its direct modern day corollary in the ultra conservative religious revolution in Iran and the terrorist activities of Moslem Extremists.

Right Wing Americans can use the following documented events for their own reasons. Left Wing Americans would just as soon such detrimental political dynamite would simply disappear into the historical woodwork.

It is ironic that Soviet historically recorded events now prove the ultimate in embarrassment to those, who in the heyday of such illustrious heroes as Lenin and Karl Marx were proud of their ethnic contributions to such a noble cause.

One informative source is **"The Communist Party of The Soviet Union"**, 1960 by Leonard Schopiro:

- Young Jewish Women in the 1880's were influenced by their radical teachers initiated protest marches against the Czar.
- Networks of intellectuals grew into broader workers' organizations.
- The Bund, a General Jewish Workers Union, by 1904, was comprised of Marxists, atheists, and anti-Capitalists, totaling an estimated number of 23,000 members.

- The formation in 1907 of the Communist Central Committee was made up of two representatives each from the Jewish, Polish, Lett Bund organizations and five representatives from the Bolsheviks, and four from the Mensheviks.
- By 1917 the Bolshevik led Russian revolution was a reality.
- At the time of the greatest protest against the Czarist cruelty, there were an estimated 800 political prisoners in all of Russia.
- The Jewish community inside Russia was only a tiny portion of the population. **Yet 52% of the Bolshevik Party was Jewish**.
- List of Jewish contingent in top circle of Bolshevik party:

Lenin, Trotsky, Lazar Kaganovich, Moltov's wife Paulina, Bulgan's wife, Nadezhda, Khrushchev's son-in-law, Lenin's grandfather, P.N. Pospelov, editor of Pravada 1940-1949, Vorshilov's wife, and Yakov Sverdlov, first Chief of State. Karl Marx was Jewish and both grandfathers were rabbis.

In the early nineteen twenties, the Russian controlled Communist attempted revolution to overthrow the German Republic failed.

In the Spanish Civil War the Republicans were in power (Communists & others). The generals revolted. It was the Republicans, who were the radical Communist element, controlled by Moscow.

In "For Whom the Bells the Toll" by Hemingway, the Republicans (Communists & others) were portrayed as the good guys (ala Gary Cooper).

In film on TV, The American Movie Channel on Thursday, September 4, 1996 was a documentary entitled **BLACKLIST TRIAL**, IN IT THE COMMUNIST ELITE IN THE FILM INDUSTRY ATTEMPT TO JUSTIFY THEMSELVES EVEN YEARS LATER. They claimed to be innocents unjustly harassed by the big bad United States Government. One said, (paraphrased), "We were just a Hollywood social club!" while commenting on communism being an international organization.

Quote by Ronald Reagan at the time of congressional hearings "A majority can be controlled by a well organized minority."

There is a very direct connection between the mindless pseudo intellectuals involved in the FEMINIST movement and the same type of intellectual speculation that led to the rise of Communist Russia, the butchery of Western European Jews and the present deplorable lack of morality in America. This writer has decided, in stolen phraseology, to damn the torpedoes, full speed ahead.

Gloria Steinem, Germaine Greer and Betty Friedan must learn not to revere what in its essence was one of the two greatest evils of the first half of the Twentieth Century and was the initial cause of the Jewish Holocaust.

Steinem extols the virtues of the young, idealistic women, not only directly involved in, but actually initiators of the Chinese Red Brigade Cultural Revolution and of the overthrow of the Shah of Iran, which established the totalitarian regime of the Ayatollah Khomeini!

Friedan quotes Dr. Spock on the meaningful lives led by Soviet women! She talks in glowing terms of the emerging Soviet puppet states of Africa and Cuba and can't wait for the glorious coming "Revolution" in America. Then the truth is revealed in:

"Short End of the Stick" "PARADE" 6/10/90

Approximately 40 million Soviet men were killed in wars and purges between 1914 & 1945. Soviet women took over almost every kind of manual labor in the country. Russian women constitute 98% street-cleaners, 66% highway workers and 90% of conveyor belt operators. 92% of Soviet women work outside their homes and according to those immigrating to the U.S. they felt totally exploited.

Germaine flippantly speaks of "Revolution" without effort and the freedom of Communism.

These "Best Educated Women" believe in the hokum of Russian Communism. No not today, because it is obvious to everyone that it is a total and absolute failure, but it was the foundation of their liberal education, the economics of their professors and the dreams of which their thoughtless brains were filled by the drivel of a certain genre of nineteen twenties and thirties pop fiction novels.

Fascism is abhorrent, so went the exciting and heroic novels of Hemingway and other American expatriate, romantic, 20th century writers. These were the writers who drank and slept their way through Paris in the 1920's and thirties. Communism was their God!

Other American writers, such as Lillian Hellman, glamorized their own lives by arbitrarily writing themselves into the circle of Communistic "freedom" fighters of Europe opposing the Fascist dictators of Spain and Germany.

Hemingway and thousands, if not tens of thousands of similarly inclined Americans, in the arts, films, university humanities and schools of economics were seduced into absolutely believing that Russian Communism was the ultimate answer to nasty Capitalism.

Many, of those seduced, most benefited from the evils of "Capitalism", but because of probable inherent guilt complexes, their greedy egos needed to express emotions of sympathy for the poor, without of course equivalent sacrifice.

This childish, selfish cadre of the hidden, sympathetic, Communistic, American underground of show business and intellectual elites were of the same mind as those who told us Picasso was brilliant and Dali was absurd. The same New York crowd that laughed and ridiculed Ayn Rand while looking the other way as Lenin and Joe Stalin murdered millions of their own people.

These same Americans hated Hitler and Franco of Spain, **not for their real inhumanities**, but because these two leaders completely halted the expansion of Russian Communism into Western Europe.

If the human race is, and such a possibility exists, logically and emotionally insane, then the likes of the Hitlers, the Stalins, the Lenins, the Steinems and the Friedans will reign in perpetuity.

If however, it is only out of environmentally developed ignorance that such is the history of mankind, then perhaps there is some small segment of hope in timely revelations of perceived reality!

COMMUNISM AND THE "JEWS"

Adolph Hitler was the only man who stood between the collapse of the German Republic, established after the loss of the First World War, and the attempted revival of the aborted German, Russian controlled Communist revolution which failed in the early Nineteen Twenties.

Hitler's followers were engaged in total street war with the German Communists. The German people were literally starving to death. The Communists in Germany were on the verge of success. Unlike Russia however, it was the strong middle class, unbelievably well disciplined, while starving to death, who sided with Hitler in his civil war against the German Communists.

The German middle class knew that if the German Communists won, then they themselves would very likely be annihilated.

The most prominent, outspoken leaders of the German and Russian Communist revolutionary efforts were radical Jewish intellectuals.

By the end of the 1940's, Stalin had reportedly murdered or otherwise through war, disposed of as many as <u>40 million Russians</u>.

Had the Communists succeeded in Germany, it is very conceivable that in order to exercise the same control over the German population that was used to create Communist Russia, as many as <u>thirty million Germans</u> would have subsequently been condemned to their own holocaust.

Hitler was paranoid about the ability of the Jewish Communist "Intellectuals" to influence public opinion and for good reason; he could see the results of their comrades in Soviet Russia. He also blamed Jewish Bankers for abandoning Germany's World War I efforts and for supporting the British efforts.

We may never know whether Hitler truly feared the entire Jewish community as being Communistically opposed to his dictatorship, or if in his worst aberrations he reasoned, if many are, then why take any risk whatsoever. Later on the Jews were simply used as scapegoats for any failure of Hitler's policies.

There were no known alternative solutions at the time. The great Western Powers, France and England, along with their industrialists and bankers, were still picking at the financial bones of the starving Germans after World War I.

Hitler was neither a sign painter nor a coward. He was less than a brilliant artist and struggling architectural student. Hitler was a five-time decorated, wounded hero of the German army in the First World War. "Mein Kampf" was not the ravings of a maniac. It was his comprehensive understanding of what ailed Germany but definitely anti-Jewish.

After the invasion of Poland by Germany in 1939, while the German Jewish communities were being persecuted and American Communists were extolling the virtues of Russia, Germany and the Soviet Russia signed a secret peace treaty and began to carve up both Eastern and Western Europe, at least on paper.

A number of books on the Jewish Holocaust reference the culpability of Americans, as well as Western Europeans. Then there is the otherwise very fine public TV series on the considerable Jewish contributions to Western civilization. Yet there remains a total reluctance to make public the well documented Jewish intellectuals who played the major leadership roles in the spread of Russian style Communist revolutions throughout Asia and Europe. They attempted to do the same thing here in the United States.

In total disregard of all this verifiable, historically accurate information, along come the three blind mice of FEMINIST brain power, little Gloria Steinem, Germaine Greer, and Betty Friedan to extol the virtues of Communism.

Gloria, in particular, enthusiastically tells us how Marxist German Communists and, especially, young Jewish women initiated the great FEMINIST movement in Germany between 1894 and 1933, exactly coinciding with their total dedication to the Russian Bolshevik Revolution.

Gloria, in sublime ignorance, tells us that those fearless female Communists were the forerunners of today's modern FEMINISTS!

Jews, while **<u>justly condemning the Holocaust</u>**, have attempted to completely obliterate from Western thought their role in the rise of Russian and Worldwide Communism. Have you ever seen the movie 'The Way We Were" starring Barbara Streisand?

In the movie a plug is made on behalf of the film's writers wherein Barbara stands before a college audience on campus and makes a heartfelt speech about the Western World being unconcerned about the fate of the Spanish during their Nineteen Thirties Civil War. She goes on to tell her campus audience how only the valiant Soviet Union was humanely coming to the rescue of the Spanish people!

Following are referenced texts to support and further document Jewish radicals and intellectuals control of Worldwide Communism and the Soviet Union's despicable part in the Spanish Civil War.

The complete and utter duplicity of the American Communism Disinformation Machine was to hide the **<u>controlling part</u>** Russia played in the 1930's Spanish Civil War. This and other documented evils are completely revealed by Stalin's master spy Oleg Tsarev. He is better known in KGB circles as Orlov. He is described as such in his co-authored book.

"Deadly Illusions" by John Costello and Oleg Tsarev, Crown publishers, Inc., N.Y., 1993.

The true story of the Russian controlled "Republican" Government losing struggle to establish a Communist State in Spain begins on page 254. Some of the following quotations should put an end to Hemmingway's martyrdom portrayals of an evil much greater than that of General Franco's.

"Stalin, while professing Soviet adherence to non-intervention, secretly approved the immediate dispatch of trained Soviet pilots to fly fighter aircraft supplied by the French. At the same time, he put off until October the sending of Soviet aircraft and tanks to Spain."

Pg. 255, "Moishe Stern. A hardened ex-comintern agent . . . assumed the passport identity of a Canadian by the name of Kleber to become the overall commander of the International Brigade."

"Although he was head of NKVD station in Madrid, General Orlov was presented to the Spanish Premier . . . as a political attaché."

"Orlov had effective control over every Soviet official."

Pg. 256, ". . . Comintern leaders from all over Europe rallied to their support and pressed Moscow to send immediate military aid." With regard to why Stalin positively responded, was because, ". . . it was determination to control the resulting Spanish government."

Pg. 257, "the International Brigade troops then arrived to help the Republican forces turn back the tide of the Nationalist (General Franco's troops) assault."

For Moscow's assistance in the Spanish civil war, the Republican Loyalists paid a heavy price. ". . . the Soviet advisers in Spain began a none too subtle process of Stalinization that was intended to bring the Republican Government and its armed forces under Moscow's direct control."

"When Moscow's bill came due, it was Orlov that Stalin looked to see that the Spanish paid up. The first 'collection' was the looting of the international treasury."

"The vaults of the Bank of Spain contained the fourth largest gold reserves in the world."

Pg. 258, As the Republicans appeared to be losing the battle for Madrid, ". . . Orlov was confronted with one of the most unusual orders of his career: Together with Ambassador Rosenberg, they were to arrange with the head of the Spanish government, Carballero, for shipment of the gold reserves of Spain to the Soviet Union."

Pg. 261, "Each of the boxes (of silver coins & gold bullion) weighed 145 lbs. . . . Orlov's final count of 7,900 boxes came out 100 boxes ahead of the official Spanish tally."

Pg. 263, ". . . he too recounted Stalin's drunken boast that Spain could kiss good-bye to its gold."

Pg. 267, He (Orlov) when faced with the accusations of his former comrade Krivitshy, "would vehemently deny any personal involvement in repressive secret police operations, nor would he concede that the NKVD in Spain was involved in brutal repression of anti-Communist opposition elements **in**, or outside of the Republican Government."

Pg. 268, "Orlov's repeated denials are, however, now exposed as lies by the Soviet archival records."

"Records finally confirm the darker side of Orlov's operations as Stalin's NKVD chief in Spain."

"The charges made by Hernandez and others that Orlov directed a Stalinist purge of Spanish Marxists and Trotshyites can now be corroborated from his actual reports and documents in the archive records."

Pg. 275, ". . . the passports of dead volunteers - especially those of the Lincoln Battalion of Americans- were seized by the NKVD as spoils of war. It was from among the surviving veterans that Orlov picked potential recruits to swell the ranks of the NKVD's international underground networks."

Pg. 282, "Trotsky and Sedov were opposed to individual terror even though, like all Leninists, they supported the exploitation of mass terror for political ends."

Pg. 285, "Yezhov directed the Executive Action Department of the NKVD . . . these were 'flying squads' of professional assassins. "

Pg. 294, "Anticipating the fate that awaited them in the basement of the Lubyanka, some of the senior officers (NKVD old Chekists) chose to hurl themselves from their office windows rather than submit to the same grim processes they themselves had employed to extract 'confessions' from their own victims."

"The trial of the Rosenbergs in 1951 and their subsequent conviction on espionage charges resulted in public furor when the death sentence was pronounced on the Jewish couple from Manhattan. To much of the public, the Rosenbergs were innocent victims, judicially sacrificed on the altar of McCarthyism."

"This impression was encouraged by outraged left-wing opinion . . . The so-called VERONA traffic was found to contain references to the Rosenbergs and their close associates . . . The Soviet transmissions had been cracked after many years of work by the US Army."

Pg. 276, "Orlov's NKVD file reveals that it was he who personally selected, trained and recruited Morris Cohen, a Jewish American from Brooklyn who had volunteered to fight with the Abraham Lincoln Battalion in Spain. A dedicated Communist and a former high school football star, Cohen was selected for training at the secret spy school".

IN SEARCH OF APOLOGIES, TIME, AUG. 22, 1994
by John Elson

Question posed by Genovese ". . . when did members of the **American Left** learn that the idealistic cause so many of them supported - the international communist movement - 'broke all records for mass murder, piling up tens of millions of corpses in less than three quarters of a century'? "

Genovese, a Marxist historian, answer, "'We knew everything essential and knew it from the beginning' - and therefore **the left was guilty of abetting unspeakable crimes."**

American Left Wing Radicals were, in effect, accomplices to mass murder. All this is in an Article by Genovese in the leftist quarterly "DISSENT". Genovese a distinguished scholar in residence at Atlanta's University Center had impeccable Leftist credentials.

"Was Stalin Necessary" by Martin Malia, US New & World Report, July 13, 1992 on "A History of Twentieth Century Russia", Harvard Press, 653 pages, by Robert Service.

"It is made clear that Lenin expected, indeed wanted the ensuing Civil War to eliminate all 'enemies' of Bolshevism." On Stalin's relationship to Lenin, Mr. Service is refreshingly unequivocal:

"Lenin's ideas of violence, dictatorship, terror, centralism, hierarchy and leadership were integral to Stalin's thinking. Lenin had bequeathed the terrorist instrumentalities to his successor:

- the Cheka
- the forced labor camps

- the one party state
- the mono-ideological mass media
- not one of these had to be invented by Stalin."

Opening a window on deceit, Commentary US News & World report, Aug. 24, 1992 Boris Yelsin opens secret archives writes James H. Billington, the Librarian of Congress

The archival material makes it clear than even before Stalin, the totalitarianism of the Soviet system began with Lenin, not Stalin. Three documents in particular relate to:

1. Lenin's lying to a Danish newspaper about any harm coming to the Czar's family as capitalist propaganda

2. An order to round up at least 100 "bloodsucking",prosperous peasants and publicly hang them as a lesson to non-cooperating peasantry

3. A similar order to murder priests as an object lesson to a village that resisted the forced closing of its churches

Documents show Lenin's government confiscated gems and cash and gave them to foreign revolutionaries to promote Communism in other countries when Russians were starving. One entry in particular, in a ledger of payments records truly stands out; **it's to that great hero of the movie "Reds", John Reed, one million rubles!**

WALL STREET JOURNAL 4/11/95 by Roger Kimiall, concerning Yale University Press publication of:

**"The Secret World of American Communism" and
"Stalin's letters to Molotov, 1925-1930."**

The books are based upon declassified documents from the Central Party Archives in Moscow. The historical accurate record reveals the distorted historical decades of conspiracy, cover ups, propaganda, vain imaginings, disinformation and outright lies.

Documents labeled "Top Secret" provide indisputable proof that the Communist Party of the United States **(CPUSA)** deployed a comprehensive underground network to recruit spies and conduct espionage activities on behalf of the Soviet Union.

"An American political organization sold itself to a totalitarian power." Confiscated gold, silver and jewels began arriving for such purposes in the U. S. as early as 1919.

Jewish industrialist, Armand Hammer, confirmed by Documentation from the "Top Secret Soviet Archives" and his father Julias, were soviet agents. discloses that the CPUSA worked directly with officers of the NKVD (later known as KGB) through an organization referred to as the BROTHER-SON NETWORK in America!

Morris Cohen, one of those involved in stealing the atomic bomb secrets, along with the Rosenbergs, was living in Moscow on a government pension. There are many revelations in these books. One confirming that members of the much mythologized Lincoln Battalion in the Spanish Civil War were "predominantly Communists and supported the Nazi-soviet pact of 1941."

Markus Wolf by F. Kempe, staff reporter, the Wall Street Journal, Berlin

The former soviet bloc's most ingenious spymaster was Markus Wolf. The Wolf family was Jewish and Communist. The family fled Nazi Germany in 1933. Markus joined the Communist party and was educated in special academies in Moscow that served as training grounds for new cadres sent to run Soviet satellites.

Great Engine of Treason 1/17/93, the Wall Street Journal, Mr. Pryce-Jones

Munzenberg was a Soviet propagandist who shrewdly perceived that if the Soviet Union were to be widely admired, the terror of its system had to be made invisible. The best way to achieve this lay in concentrating on the mistakes and failing of its enemies, first Nazism and secondly, Capitalism. Described in the book is how the likes of Hemingway, Mairaux, Sinclair Lewis and Picasso so badly wanted to believe this simple scheme that Munzenberg hardly had to do more than telephone them.

Thus he corrupted 'Intellectuals" everywhere, even catching hold in Hollywood. What looked liked independent Communist movements worldwide were completely orchestrated in Orwellian fashion by the Soviet Union.

The Master of Evasion, The Wall Street Journal,
June 2, 1997 by Heilbrunn.
Markus Wolf was the real life, prototype Russian, Master Spy for John Le Carre's fictional character, Karla! Wolf epitomizes a melancholy chapter in recent Jewish history; the embrace of Communism by many members of the German-Jewish intelligentsia who ended up as apologists for totalitarianism.

His father, Friedrich, was a leading German-Communist who came from a long line of Rabbis. The family fled Germany when the Nazis came to power in 1933. Like the Nazis, the Communists fought against the Democratic Weimar Republic of Germany. After 1945 in East Germany, at Buchenwald, the communists not the Jews are enshrined as Hitler's main target.

A Woman Who Fought Franco, Thursday Feb. 27, 1986,
San Francisco Chronicle
This was a very favorable article about the reminiscences of the wife of Robert Jordan, who was the adventurous American professor turned soldier, fighting on the side of the Spanish Republicans (Communists) against the Fascists (Nationalists). Jordan became the prototype for the principal character (played by Gary Cooper) in Hemingway's novel, "For Whom the Bells Tolls".

Don't bankroll Ex-Soviets, train them, The Wall Street
Journal, Thur., Aug. 29, 1991 by Paul Johnson

<u>**During the last decade of Czarist Russia**</u> (prior to World
War I), its growth rate was the highest in the world, even more than
Japan or the U.S. Russia was exporting 40% of its agriculture and
feeding its people better than ever before. Lenin's putsch had an
appalling aftermath. Less we forget, before Stalin, Lenin's
government slaughtered at least three million people. Lenin
destroyed the entire entrepreneurial class. Communist Party
members got the goods and luxuries according to their position, as
did the army, everyone else starved.

"WOLF OF THE KREMLIN" biography of Lazir
Kaganovich <u>**by his nephew Stuart Kahan**</u>, William & Morris,
N.Y. 1987

Lazar Kaganovich was second in command of the Soviet
Union, answerable only to Stalin. List of Jewish contingent in top
circle of Bolshevik party:

Trotsky (Lev Davidovich), Lazar Kaganovich, Moltov's wife
Paulina, Bulgan's wife, Nadezhda, Krushchev's son-in-law, Lenin
(Vlasimir Ulyanov) whose grandfather was P.N. Pospelov, editor of
Pravda 1940-1949, Vorshilov's wife and Yakov Sverdlov, first
Chief of State. Karl Marx was Jewish and both grandfathers were
rabbis.

**Trotsky stated Russian revolution could not sustain itself
unless it institutionalized worldwide revolution.**

Jews originally comprised 52% of the Bolshevik party but less
than 2% of the Russian population. Of the five million Jews in
Russia in 1895, two million immigrated to U.S.

Whenever opposition became too vocal, Kaganovich simply
yelled "anti-Semitism!" He, as Krushchev's boss, and Khrushchev
were directly responsible for the relocation famine deaths of five
million Russians.

Quotes by Kaganovich at 91 years of age (1981) to his nephew while still living in a Russian apartment as recorded in the book:

"The United States . . . is thus the foremost enemy of socialism . . . until your capitalism is destroyed and you and your people are brought into the socialist camp."

"History decrees this . . . Lenin believed that it can best be achieved through whatever means necessary to do so. We have those means."

"Need I remind you that surgery cannot be performed without destroying tissue, without spilling blood."

"You see all acts that further history and socialism are moral acts."

His nephew replied, "You believe that? You really believe it?" Reply, "Here in Russia, my dear nephew, we all believe it."

Molotov's comment to Lazar when Lazar didn't attend Yalta, was, "besides, who needs to meet two tired old men (Churchill & Roosevelt). We already know what we will get."

Lazar employed 70,000 men and women who toiled seven days a week to construct the Moscow subway, causing countless numbers of deaths. Khrushchev was his foreman.

By 1948 agents from Russian State Security were being sent in droves to America in order to enlist scientists, teachers and others to divulge the country's secrets. **The Kremlin recalled and echoed the words of Lenin.**

"The West was compromised by useful idiots".

Within days after the attempted assassination of Lenin, 1000 people were arrested and executed. **<u>There were more Russians murdered by Lenin in one day,</u> than the Czar ever had political prisoners in jail at one time.**

Lenin died at age 53 in 1924. Trotsky was in charge of the Soviet army until 1923.

During the 1920's Lazar pushed hard for a Soviet Germany. "We too struggled underground for a long time." Lazar commented that even though the German masses had been desperate in 1923, the Comintern officials in Moscow had not given sufficiently clear orders to the German Communist Party. Lenin was ill at the time and therefore the uprising of German Communists in Axony, Thuringia and Hamburg failed.

Later, in the nineteen-thirties, the world was in a deep depression. In the German elections, The Nazis obtained 6.5 million votes. The Communists received 4.5 million votes.

In 1936, Moscow ordered the French Communist Party to stage massive strikes in France to topple the government. The effort failed. Meanwhile in Spain, the Communists gained control of the government under the guise of calling themselves "Republicans". Civil War broke out and General Franco defeated the Communists (Republicans) who were supported and controlled by Russia.

The Cheka established in 12/20/1917 quickly transformed itself into a political state police force committed to extermination of all opposition. Quote by Felix Dzerzhinsky, its director, appointed by and reporting directly to Lenin, **"We stand for organized terror even if it sometimes falls upon heaps of the innocent."**

That was exactly what Lenin wanted. In 1922 the name, Cheka, was changed to GPU & again in 1924 to OGUP, today known as the KGB.

Kaganovich, on Stalin's many purges, "The merest slip can be outright suicide. People live in perpetual fear of informers who listen and report what they have heard. **It is ten times worse than the days of the Czar."** From1926-1929, Lazar was talking to Stalin on the phone six times a day, meeting in person twice a day.

In 1934 the "Great Terror" began. Yagoda and Kaganovich were put in charge. Millions of loyal Russian citizens were demoted, arrested, sent off to forced labor camps or just plain murdered. That purge lasted until 1939.

DARK-STAR Novel, by Alan Furst, Houghton, Mifflin Co, Boston

The novel based upon a conversation in Paris in 1937 between Soviet Intelligence officer, L.L. Feldbin, alias Alexander Orlov and his cousin Zinovy Katsnelson, a state security commissar for the Ukraine.

Until 1933 when Hitler officially took office in Germany, Russia and Germany secretly conspired to ignore the treaty ending

World War I, concerning Germany's agreement not to rearm. Junker aircraft and munitions for Germany were being built in Russia. German fighter pilots were trained in Russia. Russian wheat traveled west and German technology traveled east.

Russian freighters delivered 300,000 shells plus gunpowder and fuses to Germany disguised as pig iron and aluminum. All this went on for at least 12 years. At the time, Moscow believed the Russian Communists would eventually control Germany, not the Nazi's.

The NKVD and the GPU were staffed with thousands of old Bolsheviks (mostly Jews), all concentrated in positions of power, including the Foreign Department that handled most of the secret and sophisticated tasks. Stalin at the time was trying to get closer to Hitler and at the same time purge the old Bolsheviks. The purge was intended to get rid of those who knew too much and knew where the bodies were buried.

THE COLLAPSE OF THE WEIMAR REPUBLIC
BY DAVID ABRAM, HD361G35A27
EXCERPTS

"The Nazis were a radical, 'antisystem' but also anti-Marxist movement."

Communism and the Jews
"The Mystical Body of Christ in the Modern World"
by Rev. Denis Fahey

"According to data furnished by the Soviet press, out of 556 important functionaries of the Bolshevik State (1918-1919 . . . 457 were Jews"

Six men led the Bolshevik revolt in Russia, Lenin, Trotsky, Zinoviev, Kamenev, Sverdlev and Lunacharsky. Five of these men were Jews. Their master plan was written by Karl Marx, son of a Jewish Rabbi.

Michal Hrushevsky in his "**History of the Ukraine**",
Yale University Press 1941 states:

"In 1897 was founded the Bund, the Union of Jewish Workers in Poland and Lithuania . . . they engaged in revolutionary activity on a large scale, and their energy made them the spearhead of the (Communist) party."

On the sealed train from Germany to Moscow carrying Lenin and his followers, "Out of a list of 165 names published, 23 are Russian, 3 Georgian, 4 Armenians, 1 German and 129 Jewish" according to "Surrender of an Empire" by N. H. Webster, 1931, pg. 77.

On Pg. 73 according to the same source, "At about the same time, Trotsky (Jew) arrived from United States followed by over 300 Jews from the East End of New York."

ELSIE CHAITKEN was her name. Elsie, at the time I knew her, was about 65 years old and was caring for her 100-year-old mother in an apartment located on Cedar Street in Chicago, Illinois. Elsie was Jewish and the daughter of the World War II owners of the famous Pete Kelley's nightclub in Chicago, one of the all time great nightclubs in the United States.

Elsie would have Judy (later, my wife) and myself over for Thanksgiving dinner. Elsie operated a typing service out of her apartment. Occasionally, I would help Elsie with setting up telephones and her computer when things went awry.

Elsie loved to reminisce about the nightclub, the famous acts and what went on in Chicago during World War II. I never tired of her storehouse of fabulously entertaining stories and remembrances.

Once, at the end of one such story, I asked Elsie if many of her Jewish friends and acquaintances had been Communists in those days. Her reply was very emphatic, **"We all were"**! This remark pertained to show business and Jewish intellectuals, **not the average hard working American Jew.**

69

Robert John, **<u>Behind the Balfour Declaration</u>**

". . . in March 1917 to celebrate the revolution which had then taken place, Rabbi Stephen Wise, who had succeeded Brandeis as chairman of the American Provisional Zionist Committee after Brandeis's appointment to the Supreme Court, said:"

"I believe that of all the achievements of my people, none has been nobler than the part the sons and daughters of Israel have taken in the great movement which has culminated in free Russia."

V. THE BLACK AMERICAN MYTH

Next in priorities, through the utilization of common sense, is recognition that not since the great social schemes of Lyndon Baines Johnson has any other crazy American social justice rhetoric propelled black Americans more swiftly on the road to depressive poverty than has the modern day FEMINIST movement.

Can black Americans gain a lasting piece of the enormous American apple pie? Only if they start by surrendering their most cherished nurtured folklore concerning the white Anglo-Saxon male. Such a sacrifice of emotional comfort might permit them to enter the perceived "real" world of this country. It's the same folklore that FEMINISTS have used to berate the white Anglo-Saxon male in order to build their crazy quilt patchwork of FEMININE nonsense.

There is no better route, for a less than auspicious new beginning, then for American blacks to come to grips with the historical truth concerning African slavery. That single persistent myth permitting multitudinous vested interests to manipulate the black American population is:

THAT THROUGH INHERITED RESPONSIBILITY, THE WHITE ANGLO-SAXON MALE IS THE "ROOT" CAUSE OF ALL THE BLACK MAN'S FAILURES AND PROBLEMS.

It is vital to the best interest of black Americans that they learn to assimilate the truth of their origins, who is responsible, and why slavery actually ceased to exist.

The "Roots" of African slavery lay in ancient Egypt, Palestinian and Roman times. Slavery in Africa is over 3000 years old. In the 2nd and 3rd century AD, the great apologist for the Catholic Church was a brilliant Negro philosopher, the African St. Augustine, who was indirectly responsible for the destruction of the Gnostic gospels.

After the fall of the Holy Roman Empire, until at least the l7th century AD, all of Africa was controlled by the Negro tribes and those Arab nations that were indigenous or contiguous to the continent. By the l7th century there were a small and insignificant number of white Dutch Boers who settled on the southeastern coast of Africa. After years of fighting the Zulu tribe for supremacy, the Boers eventually founded the nation of South Africa.

Prior to that time, **the Zulus conquered and subjugated hundreds of southern African tribes, and in more than one instance, committed genocide along the way.**

With this cursory historical background it would be helpful for black Americans to make reference to a map of Africa and the Middle East. Why, because the next statement to be made will be psychologically shocking to black Americans. Hopefully, it will be permanently engraved on their consciousness.

Slavery in Africa and the Middle East was indigenous to the continent!

Slavery existed in biblical times, during the occupation of the Romans and on into the l9th Century AD! By definition, the white "Anglo-Saxon" only became briefly involved thousands of years later for approximately one hundred years; even then as only the last link in the historical horrible business.

Except for the rarest of incidents, the popular image of any human beings other than black Africans and Arabs, let alone white Anglo-Saxons, unless invited, traveling around Africa rounding up slaves, raping women and killing children is absolutely ludicrous. White "Anglo-Saxons" were thousands of miles distant, separated from Africa by a number of seas, the Atlantic Ocean and millions of unfriendlies.

During the brief period of institutionalized slavery in the United States of America (1789-1865), there were undoubtedly thousands of atrocities committed against black slaves, imported from Africa.

In comparison to **atrocities committed by other black Africans** and Arabs, on the whole, American black slaves were treated significantly better. Not because Americans were more moral or Christian-like, but because it was simply good business.

One of the most important and historically documented works on African slavery has been written by de Wismes, "Nantes Et Le Temps Des Negriers", published by France-Empire. Unfortunately, the book is in the French language.

A less readable, but English language text, is "The African Slave Trade from the 15th to the 19th Century", #92-3-1Q 1672-5, UNESCO Books, 1180 Avenue of the Americas, New York, N. Y. 10076.

The Le Baron Armel de Wismes has direct family knowledge of the slave trade. His residence is in close proximity to the only two cities outside Africa, itself, which maintain historical museums devoted to African slavery. The two cities are Nantes and Bordeaux. Both cities are in France.

It is left to the imagination of the well educated and politically sophisticated American blacks as to what means will be found to teach the truth to their less fortunate brothers and sisters. This will free them from the bondage of ignorance that has been used to keep them from assuming complete responsibility for their own well being in these United States of America. The basic truths are:

<u>FOR MORE THAN 400 YEARS BLACK AFRICANS CAPTURED, ENSLAVED AND SOLD OTHER BLACKS! BLACKS, ARABS AND PORTUGUESE PENNED UP AND BRED BLACK SLAVES!</u>

Following is a brief summary of facts gleaned from the historical references cited earlier: Keep in mind that the United States did not exist in the 15th, 16th or 17th centuries.

During that same period Anglo-Saxons did not populate America.

The modern day era of black African slavery began when Moslems conquered Constantinople disrupting spice trade to Europe from India and the East. By 1441 Portuguese explorers, looking for safer sea routes for their spice shipments first purchased black slaves from black Africans for resale in Europe. The slaves were sold as curiosities throughout Europe, not as manual laborers. Profits from slaves helped offset losses in the spice trade.

Columbus did not even "discover" America until 1492 and from then until well into the 18th century, Spain was a dominant force in America.

In fact, until at least the middle of the 17th century, Spain was a dominant force in Europe.

The thirteen original colonies of the United States freed themselves from England; but until 1803, when they purchased from the <u>French</u> all of the Louisiana territory that extended all the way to Canada, at least 1/3 of America was controlled by the French.

Within 128 years of Columbus's "discovery" (1492-1620), the Spanish brought diseases, wars and famines to the New World, reducing the Indian population in the Americas from 100 million to less than 10 million!

<u>**One hundred years before the pilgrims landed on Plymouth Rock,**</u> all of Europe became intoxicated by shipments of new and exciting food products from the Americas. Such fabulous delights as chocolate, vanilla, corn, tomatoes, potatoes, coffee, and tobacco addictively excited the European palates.

Slavery was not about Christianity or Anglo-Saxon enslavement of Africans. Slavery was international trade, African tribal warfare, jealousy, enormous profits for black and Arab slave traders, and the manual labor required to plant and harvest crops.

All of Europe, with the exception of Czarist Russia, speculated in the slave trade. Profits from buying slaves from **black** and Arab slave traders could be as much as 300% to 1,000% return on one's investment.

Everybody got in on the act. Typical European investors ranged from little old ladies, farmers, merchants, and titled princes to such unlikely models of virtue as the French philosopher, Voltaire!

Ship captains purchased slaves from African traders and holding pen wholesalers. The slaves were sold in North America as farm labor. The ships were then loaded with fresh food delicacies and delivered to the European market. The ships then returned to Africa to buy more slaves. The unholy cycle was endlessly repeated from the **1500's AD** until 1860.

From 1451 through 1860 there were 12 million to 25 million Africans sold into slavery.

Captured and sold almost entirely by Africans, Portuguese and Arabs!

WHAT TERRIBLE PART DID BLACK AFRICA ITSELF PLAY IN THIS HUMAN TRAGEDY? BLACK AFRICANS INITIATED BLACK SLAVERY AND PERPETUATED IT!

THE MAJOR CAPTURER AND SELLER FOR 400 YEARS OF BLACK SLAVES WERE NEGRO TRIBES DEEP IN THE INTERIOR OF AFRICA!

BLACK SLAVES CAPTURED BY AFRICAN BLACKS WERE SOLD TO BLACK AND ARAB SLAVE TRADERS.

THE SLAVE TRADERS DROVE THEIR BLACK SLAVES IN BARBARIC FASHION FROM THE INTERIOR OF AFRICA TO THE SHORES OF WESTERN AFRICA. MILLIONS DIED ALONG THE WAY, LONG BEFORE ANY SLAVES WERE PLACED ABOARD SHIP.

BLACK SLAVES WERE HELD IN TRADING FORTS ALL ALONG THE WESTERN COAST OF AFRICA, WHERE BLACK TRIBES, ARABS AND PORTUGUESE ACTUALLY BRED SLAVES IN CAPTIVITY.

THERE ARE UNSPEAKABLE HORRORS WELL DOCUMENTED AS TO THE PENNING UP OF BLACK AFRICANS BY BLACK AFRICANS, ARABS AND PORTUGUESE SLAVERS TO BE MATED, REPRODUCE, MATED AND REPRODUCE OVER AND OVER AGAIN!

ENTIRE GENERATIONS OF BLACK SLAVES WERE BRED FOR PROFIT, DEPRIVING THEM OF PARENTS, HISTORICAL ROOTS OR A COHESIVE LANGUAGE.

SO-CALLED "ANGLO-SAXONS" WERE THOUSANDS OF MILES AWAY FROM THE POINT IN TIME AND PLACE, WHEN THE MAJORITY OF BLACK AFRICAN SLAVES LOST THEIR HERITAGE!

Once the majority of American Negroes accept the truth of these historically documented facts, all past techniques for manipulating the American Negro will be passé. New ones, of course, will arise, but at least those illusions of historical gibberish pitting blacks against whites in America will evaporate.

Before summarizing the purpose and relationship of this chapter to the harebrained schemes of the latest American FEMINIST movement, it is incumbent upon me to fill in the gap from the early 1800's until the present day to further dispel additional myths that have been used to manipulate black Americans.

It would be well to once again see the TV presentation that was shown at 3 PM Pacific Coast Time, CH. 28 that is CH. 50 KCSM PBS SAN MATEO ON FRIDAY APRIL 8TH, 1988.

TITLE: "THE AFRICANS"

Lincoln's original solution (simply and plainly due to economic reasons and to defuse the possibility of a Civil War over Federal vs States Rights) was to consider shipping all slaves to the Caribbean islands or return them to Africa.

About midway through the Civil War, Lincoln proposed to free the slaves as a military and political tactic to negotiate the end of the war.

After the Civil War, discrimination and segregation were perpetuated in the south by the Democrats.

The current dependency of the American black population on the Federal Government has been the ruination of their emergence as an economic force in the United States.

School busing, using black and white children as laboratory rats in a social experiment, has had disastrous results on the education of both races. Black children and particularly young black males are, on average, totally without arithmetic or language skills.

The same mistake made by black Americans in the 1960's in the field of education is now being made by blacks in regard to their belief in the FEMINIST movement today. By appealing to black America's belief that the white "Anglo-Saxon" male is the heart of the problem, despite irrefutable historical evidence to the contrary, a majority of American blacks may be taking their final step into unrelenting poverty for generations to come!

Black irrational response to the passage of the Civil Rights Act was to embark on a useless, RELENTLESS rampage of violence throughout their neighborhoods. This type of intentional self-destruction was not unlike similar activities conducted by Chinese Red Guards, so romantically eulogized by the FEMINISTS.

An article in the Wall Street Journal titled "Mao's Orphans" contained interviews with previous student Red Guards who are now adults. Almost without exception, these people have grown up without any skills and do not fit China's economic requirements.

More importantly, the adults who were harassed by those young people do not trust them now that they have become adults. The results are quoted as follows:

"As mature adults, these people should have been the backbone of China's modernization. But millions left school to wage revolution and many never came back. Now, without skills or educations, they watch their younger brothers and sisters leapfrog them to the top."

Sound familiar? It should. Today young black men are not learning to read or write while young Jewish, Christian and other women are leapfrogging over all black males!

Not only are black Americans repeating their mistakes of the 1960's, 1970's, 1980's and 1990's, but they are supporting the very FEMINIST movement that increases the black male rate of unemployment!

American industry has not stood still for twenty years. The U.S. requirements for increased technical competence have skyrocketed in the 1980's and continue to escalate, even today. Only those with very high skills in language, mathematics, computers and science will, on the average, reach economic well being.

Most low paying jobs will be in the service businesses. There is NO EASY WAY black Americans can leap ahead through the passage of ERA; instead they have jumped off a cliff.

Their only means of "getting even" is the long tortuous road back from single family homes and a totally Failed Public School Educational System. Blacks must instill absolute discipline in their neighborhoods and in their children's educational systems so that their children learn reading, writing and arithmetic until each child, regardless of age, meets non-doctored proficiency standards.

Epidemic, out-of-wedlock black birthrates in the inner cities is culturally devastating to black prosperity and a drag on the entire US economy.

THERE IS NO OTHER WAY!

The radical American FEMINIST movement joined tacit forces with the radical black revolutionaries of the 1960's. What do the black youth of today have to show for that mess? First the FEMINISTS aided in the destruction of the black family unit. Today they work even harder to destroy the fabric remnants of the American family for blacks and other Americans.

What did a leading black journalist have to say about the destructive influence of "NOW" on her black sisters? In a Detroit

News article dated **October 12, 1983**, June Brown urged black women to the following course of action in direct opposition to "NOW".

<u>"Marriage success is the first essential for black women."</u>

"As a rule, white women hold far more aces in the marriage game than black women do."

"In the black community a successful marriage and a good husband are the best prize a career woman can have."

"Select a career that will help them meet the kind of men they want for husbands."

"No woman, black or white, should be foolish enough to give her entire life to a career."

"In the end, nothing in a career woman's life is more important than a successful marriage."

"And as more white women have babies out of wedlock and fall into poverty, a successful marriage will become essential for them also."

Everything that the FEMINIST "NOW" movement is attempting to politically accomplish in the United States is diametrically opposed to the best interests of black Americans! Yet similar to their radical black brothers in the 1960s, their black sisters are, even today, some of the most outspoken women in the "NOW" political movement. The very black women whose long-term search for true social and economic justice is being crushed by "NOW".

The modern American upper class Jewish and other white FEMINIST of the "Smith Girl" mentality are preaching free love, thus swelling the ranks of the welfare roles. Furthermore the "Smith Girls" were espousing the revolutionary zeal of the Chinese Red Brigade, the crazy Iranian revolutionaries, and the sterling young maidens of Russian and German Communism. They tacitly encouraged black youth to take what they wanted from their own neighborhoods.

"NOW" the "Girls of Smith", devilishly, under the guise of equal rights, desire to nail shut, out of complete selfishness, the economic coffin of black America.

The United States, from 1964 through today, spent more money than all nations combined in the total history of mankind to "rehabilitate" black Americans.

By the brute force of expenditures the United States government attempts to force Negroes into the main stream of American economics. The obscene amounts of taxpayer money (both black and white) devoted to racial equality first doubled, then tripled and then tripled again. Simultaneously the FEMINIST reached a peak of shrillness harping for the necessity of "equal rights" for women!

Never, as a part of near bankrupt generosity, have blacks and white American women been poorer; all this because of the crazy schemes of the Federal Government and their subsequent pandering to the stupid priority agenda of the upper and middle class FEMINISTS, today's liberated women.

How tragic have been the results of all this glorious state of social welfare and awareness? Even as early as the August 13, 1984, an issue of U. S. News and World Report revealed some frightening statistics, enumerating the depth of human tragedy in America.

THE FASTEST RISING IMPOVERISHED GROUP in the United States since 1970 has been <u>Head of the Household White Women</u>.

As a class, the percentage of the white population in poverty had risen from 8% to 12% in just 14 years, since the bulk of this increase has been attributed to head of the household white women, their real poverty is even substantially greater. This means <u>those white women added</u> to the <u>poverty roles has increased more than 50% in 14 years</u>! **This was in 1984.** Today those statistics are even more staggering.

Blacks should not revel in this demise of prosperity in the ranks of white women. As the percentage of white women escalates the poverty roles, there will be even less support for black poverty.

Yet, despite the obscene amount of money devoted to black poverty over the last forty or fifty years, the latest score card announces that as a percentage of their population, black poverty has increased from 31% to 36%, a 17% increase in just 14 years.

This increase cannot be blamed on the ex-President, Ronald Reagan. Had a Democratic President stayed in office and increased the amount of money available, inflation would have continued to rise more rapidly and the results would have remained the same or possibly worsened because real income would have fallen further.

The simple truth is:

ALL THAT HAS BEEN SAID AND DONE IN THE PAST AND IN THE PRESENT, BY GOVERNMENT, IN REGARD TO POVERTY IS COMPLETELY WRONG!

Just as all the arguments and predictions made by the FEMINIST "Smith Girls" are WRONG!

The amount of money spent on the arms race is a completely separate problem. And in the past, there has been no statistical correlation between decreased military expenditures and increased expenditures on poverty.

In fact, almost without exception, no matter what percentage of the National Budget has been devoted to the Military, the number of those at or below the poverty level in the United States has continued to rise.

Here we are almost five decades later, 60% of an individual's lifetime, having spent more money on armaments and more on poverty than all the nations together in the history of the world, only to find that we have institutionalized poverty as a way of life.

<u>On the sole basis of past experience</u>, if we entirely disbanded our military and infinitely increased our expenditures on poverty we would be:

A TOTALLY POOR, DEFENSELESS NATION!

Any organization that encourages white women to enter the American labor force is automatically detrimental, in the extreme, to the best interests of the black American male. As more and more white women are suckered into the nutty fantasy world of "NOW", more and more white women will enter the world of poverty!

On average, these white women are better educated and have more direct and favored access to the business world, even at the low end of the job spectrum. These white women have superior arithmetical and language skills compared to the average black male or female. Efficiency in the American business world is practically non-existent in the office and clerical functions, to say nothing of middle and top management.

The only relatively efficient workers are direct labor operators and farmers. Direct labor operators are being replaced by robots. Computers are replacing extremely inefficient office, clerical and middle management people.

The vast bulk of "MEANINGFUL CAREER JOBS" are in low paying service industries such as fast food restaurants, door to door sales, computer clerical operators, etc. The competition for these jobs will be ferocious. The winner will undoubtedly be the poor white woman; not that it will help her much.

There have always been very simple (not easy) and direct methods for eliminating poverty in America that could undo all the misery induced by the immoral and unconscionable screwy schemes of the Federal Government and the Betty Friedans of this world.

The money spent over the past fifty years by the Federal Government (not including unemployment payments by the states) for subsidizing poverty in the United States is in the neighborhood of several trillion dollars (a very, very expensive neighborhood).

Even one trillion dollars is equivalent to an average of $100,000 per black family in America, four people per family (most often that family is composed of a single black female and two or three children). If that money had been given, over the same period of time, directly to all black families in the form of tax free municipal bonds, each black family in America could have an annual tax free income of from 5,000 to $10,000 a year and a net worth of $100,000.

Until black Americans realize the road to "Success" in America is their responsibility, not the government's, not the "Anglo-Saxon" white male and certainly not "NOW", no amount of complaining or self-righteous indignation over civil rights is going to effortlessly lift black Americans to prosperity in a very competitive society.

First, all black children must master the basics of reading, writing and arithmetic. Then they must still face the long tough road of acquiring marketable skills. If black Americans continue to rely on the Federal Government and "NOW" for economic survival, let alone parity, then black Americans will continue to, not only ruin their own future and the future of their children, but sow the seeds for the ruination of their children's children.

The nation as a whole and especially Blacks must condemn out-of-wedlock pregnancies!

VI. WHITE ANGLO-SAXON MALES

Who are these white devils that control every aspect of our lives, force their women to live in nine room concentration camp homes, oppress the Jews, enslave the Blacks and disdain those of Hispanic origin throughout the Western world?

In mythology they are a singular dominant white, male species with a line of ancestors traced unerringly and homogeneously back to the original Caucasians. Historically documented evidence gives lie to this ridiculous mythology. Once and for all is eliminated the psychological crutches of those who cannot otherwise come to terms with the true competitive nature of the American Democratic Republic.

For those unafraid of the truth, although mislead through ignorance, it is a simple matter to verify the cursory historical information revealed throughout this chapter. One might begin by checking such diverse sources as, The Races of Europe by Ripley, African Kingdoms by Lucy Mair, The Myth of the Jewish Race by Patai and Wing, and Races of Mankind (Public Affairs pamphlets,

1943) by Benedict and Weltfish. Further independent study can of course be left to the ingenuity of the reader.

What is the long postponed answer to the enigmatic question of just who comprises the group of racially arrogant, white Anglo-Saxon males? The group, according to FEMINISTS and Blacks, that rule and ruin American Society, has its refreshing and novel solution in recorded anthropology!

By definition, RACES are basically three in nature, with a possible fourth thrown in for good measure. There is little or no correlation between RACE and Nationality, nor between RACE and Language. There is a correlation between Nationalities and Language. Within a given Nationality, RACES and Languages are intermixed.

The three RACES of mankind are NEGROID, MONGOLOID and CAUCASIAN. The sometime fourth, argumentatively, is designated as ABORIGINAL. Aborigines include those by the same name in Australia, the Pygmies of Africa and South America, the Brits and the ancient and all but forgotten Firblogs. Usually, but not always, Aborigines are otherwise classified as NEGROID.

One of the more interesting conclusions, generally agreed upon by most anthropologists, is the fact that language plays no significant role in terms of racial lines of ancestry! The reason for eliminating language as one acceptable criteria of racial origin is due to the fact that too many anthropologists, whom have taken that line of attack in the past, have been proven erroneous in their conclusions by their peers.

In the simplest and most basic definition of Race, someone absolutely Black in color pigmentation, having no genetic characteristics remotely related to the MONGOLOID, or CAUCASIAN Races, would be classified as NEGROID. One of the three pure color pigmentations (Black, white or yellow) <u>coupled with the absence of any genetic characteristic remotely related to either of the other two RACES</u> would be as close to RACIAL PURITY as one could hope to achieve.

With regard to speaking of the Mongoloid race as being of the color referred to as yellow is somewhat misleading. The designation has more to do with the shape of their skulls and facial features as can be found throughout Asia.

Conversely, **regardless of color of skin pigmentation**, dominant genetic characteristics could very well classify an individual as predominantly descendant from the race of their most dominant genetic qualities. A blue-black Asian might very well be classified as CAUCASIAN, MONGOLOID, or NEGROID depending upon the dominant genetic strain of his or her ancestors. Those ancestors whose overall features and skeletal frame coupled with lineage, best describe the physical consolidation of that individual, **not necessarily the color of skin.**

The probability of a significant number of pure, unadulterated NEGROID, MONGOLOID, or CAUCASIAN individuals residing in America is for all practical purposes ZERO!

With all of this rudimentary information secure in your mind, let's look historically from whence came the evil white Anglo-Saxon male.

History and anthropology trace the beginning of the original Caucasian race, which later appeared in Europe, to the Near East and India. For the purposes of early cataloging, Caucasians were further stratified into Nordics (fair skinned, blue eyed, tall and long headed), Alpines (stocky, broad headed, medium build), and Mediterraneans (slender, darker, and long headed).

Aryans, Jews, Arabs, Tartars and Zulus are all broadly classified as groups, each group having something in common. <u>None of these groups are RACES</u>. Aryans, for example, are a very broad group of nationalities, whose similarities of language and Indo-European cultures led to those peoples being referred to as Aryans.

Jews, contrary to common belief, have no claim to racial purity, and at best can be referred to as a culturally religious integrated group of white, Negro and Mongolian heritages. Diversity abounds throughout the Old Testament.

The "typical Jewish type" of European is a relatively influential minority of Jews who have a distinctive appearance, not because of their Jewish religious persuasion, but because of their southern Italian origins.

Appearance wise, these Jews have little or no common genetic characteristics with Negroid or Mongolian Jews. In fact, a discovery of an entire Negro Jewish sect (isolated for hundreds of years in Ethiopia), when rescued from starvation by the Jews of Israel, the sect did not even know there existed other Jews in the world; let alone those who were predominantly Caucasian or Mongoloid.

Webster's Unabridged Dictionary's fourth definition of "Mediterranean" is:

"4. in ethnology, designating or of one of the three main divisions of the Caucasian, or white race: term used to denote typically long-headed, short, olive skinned peoples living around the Mediterranean Sea, including ancient Iberian, Ligurian, Pelasgian, and Hamitic peoples and their descendants."

Webster's definition of "Hamitic" is:

"1.   of or relating to Ham or the Hamites."

"2.   designating or of a group of African languages related to the Semitic languages and including ancient Egyptian (surviving, from 3400 B. C. , as the religious language Coptic), ancient Libyan, the modern Berber dialects, and the Cushitic dialects of Ethiopia and eastern Africa."

3.   Webster's definition of "Ham" is:"in the Bible, Noah's second son, traditionally the ancestor of African peoples: Gen. X. 6-20."

From loosely defined biblical description, Jews were possibly very small in stature. David's slaying of the giant Goliath may have only been one of perspective, from the smaller man's point of view. Similarly, the exodus of slaves from Egypt included large numbers of other nationalities, not just Semites.

Zulus of Africa conquered many tribes in southern Africa and were not saints when it came to breeding habits. Germans, Frenchmen, Americans, Italians, Berbers, Nigerians, Russians, Iranians, British, Irish, French, Mexicans, Spanish and the Aztec Indians are NATIONALITIES, not RACES. Any pureness of race within these nationalities is not only less than plausible, it is ridiculous!

Germans and Frenchmen share many characteristics of the Alpine Caucasian, with a substantial influence in their northern most provinces of Nordic Caucasian types. The influx of slaves, since at least 1500 A D, not to mention the black G. I. of the Second World War, or the mixing of French and Algerians, represent only the tip of the iceberg of the <u>total interbreeding of RACES</u> over the recorded millenniums.

A fast anthropological, loosely jointed trip through history will provide some general idea of the cross-fertilization of RACES and Nationalities, long before we approach 1776 and the mythology of the white Anglo-Saxon male.

Cro-Magnons from Europe bred with migrating peoples from the East and Southwest crossing Europe intermittently throughout recorded history. Such interracial breeding took place, almost unceasingly, throughout the Asian, the North African and the European continents.

Phoenicians over the centuries plied trading expeditions throughout the Mediterranean. Romans went to Spain and later the British Isles. Huns swept in from Asia (yes, that's correct - Asia, not Germany), overran central Europe and crushed the Holy Roman Empire!

Tartars came from the East. Followers of Islam captured all of North Africa, invaded Spain, and held it for hundreds of years, even crossing the Pyrenees into France. Nationalities, not race, loosely began to describe Europeans from the mixture of Cro-Magnons, Slavs, Mongols, Africans, Celts, Saxons, Teutons and most anybody else who migrated throughout Europe.

In recent history, after World War I, Germans and Czech's along a common border intermarried so quickly that today, only 90 years later, along that border they cannot be distinguished in appearance by nationality, let alone something as vague as RACE. Yet to this day, each nationality as a group has no love for the other.

Few nationalities during their heyday in history were more brutal and oppressive than were the Mexicans. Aztec intermarriage with lesser tribes bred an indigenous Mexican culture that eventually succumbed to brutal Spanish conquest. Now both Spanish and Mexican immigrants to America cry discrimination.

If you happen to be fair-haired, tall, long headed and hail from Europe, anthropologically speaking, <u>you are Nordic, not Aryan</u>!

If you are Spanish, just for starters you are kin to the Berbers from Morocco, Algiers and Tunis. You and the Portuguese, are part of the historical migration known as the Iberian connection. Your recent ancestors were allied to Europeans, culturally.

Geographically the Spanish were in close contact politically and militarily to North Africa and separated from France by the Pyrenees. Spain was the four lane super highway of the middle ages from Africa to Europe. The Spaniards were genetically allied with the inhabitants of Africa, usually those north of the Sahara, from the Red Sea to the Atlantic Ocean.

The beautiful "honey-brown eyed" women of southwestern Spain are testimony to the tremendous influence of the <u>African Moors</u>; then of course there are the curly headed, <u>dark complexion Basques </u>of Spain.

The <u>Basques</u> had a language similar to that of the Lapps, Finns, Hungarians, and of all people, the <u>Aborigines of Asia and the Americas.</u> And even stranger yet, according to the Roman historian, Tacitus, through language there was a direct <u>cultural link between the Caledonians</u> and <u>the Germans</u>. Caledonians were ancient people who inhabited Scotland and <u>were considered Aborigines</u>!

Italy, in contrast to Spain, had an early number of Teutonic invaders, the Cimbri, Goths, Ostrogoths, Visigoths, Saxons, Engles, and Lombards. Devastating as were their invasions, in actual number they were insignificant. The peasant stock of northwestern Italy is believed to be descendant of a people known as Ligurians. Ligurians were the people as early as 700 BC who are believed to have composed the toughest of the Roman battle legions.

Originally it was the Ligurians who anthropologists thought came over the Alps and entered Central Europe. Later it was discovered that it actually was the broad head Celts. The Celts were descendants of the earlier Umbrians, who themselves were Aryans!

The Etruscans, later known as Romans had earlier conquered the Umbrians. The Estruscans ancestry is traced to the Tyrrhenians of Asia Minor and the Raseni tribes of the Alps.

Off the coast of Italy lie the isles of Sicily and Sardinia, occupied at one time or another by the Sicani, the Siculi, the Fenici, Greeks, Romans, Albanians, Vandals, Goths, Saracens, Normans, Spanish and French. Boy! And you think we have problems!

Interesting, but what does all this have to do with Anglo-Saxon male domination of today's FEMINISTS, American Negroes and Hispanics? Patience is its own reward and RACIAL CORRELATION is beginning to seep into your consciousness, as we travel through time and continents.

For thousands of years there were intermarriages of blacks, whites and Mongolian people. We see the historical record of migration from Africa, Asia, and Asia Minor into Spain, Portugal and Italy, as well as flurries across the Pyrenees into France and Central Europe.

In numerical sense, all this time the British Isles with its ABORIGINAL stock of Brits (that's right ladies - ABORIGINES) remained relatively undisturbed. Then in rapid sequence, the British Isles were invaded by the Romans, the Jutes, Saxons, Engles, and finally the Normans (originally descended from the Nordic tribes of Swedes and Danes).

The Jutes, Saxons and Engles hit the shores of good old Britain over at least a three hundred year period, from about 300 A. D. into 600 AD, by which time their invasions had reached into upper Ireland. So anti-Saxon were the Brits that for nearly two hundred years if a Brit had to so much as a drink from a Saxon cup, it would first be cleansed in boiling water and then thoroughly scoured.

Just about the time the Brits, Saxons, Jutes, and Engles settled down to all the comforts of home and began speaking to each other, along come the DANES. The Danes settled down to the serious business of conquering the British Isles in about 850 A. D.

Not to be outdone, the Normans (under William the Conqueror) completed the Norman conquest of the British Isles in 1200 AD. Of course, with all these little family tiffs being sorted out, it took about 400 more years for everybody to get acquainted! Just in time for all the new neighbors in England to gang together and beat the hell out of all those who by then called themselves Irish!

Hopping, skipping and jumping a couple of hundred years across the Atlantic Ocean, we find ourselves in the middle of the American Revolution. The British were entrenched in Massachusetts, Maryland and Georgia. The French were in Texas and throughout the Louisiana Territories. The Mexicans were in

Texas. The French Huguenots were in the Carolinas, the Spanish in Florida and California, and the jolly Russians in Alaska.

The British were only one of many nationalities that imported slaves into the Americas from the African slave traders. But here is the real kicker, who in the hell were the British? And the anthropologists tell us one thing for certain:

<u>THEY WERE NOT ANGLO-SAXONS!</u>

It is questionable that the Saxons were ever really in control at anytime in England. After 400 AD, until the time of the Danish and Norman invasions of the British Isles, those in control were of course, The ENGLES. How else, one might ask, does the country become known as <u>ENGLAND</u>, certainly not so called by the Saxons.

But wait a minute, what about the original Brits? You know as in <u>Brit</u>ain! Well, let's just say they had one hellava underground organization. The island group, England, Scotland and Ireland, are called the British Isles, and it was the <u>Brit</u>ish Empire for 400 years, not the Saxon Isles, or the country of Saxland, or the Saxon Empire. And the original Brits were ABORIGINES!

By 600 AD, the genetic mixture was about 50% Brits and 50% Nordic; later the Norman Conquest diluted that mixture, in its broadest sense, by another 20%.

But what does that matter? Shrilly shout the FEMINISTS, blacks and Hispanics! There were plenty of whites; be it Engles, Danes, Normans, Jutes or Saxons. We're mad as hell and we have to blame someone for our failures, so let's call them all Germanic tribes, and so what if they're 30% ABORIGINE (Negroid).

Those dirty no good Germans. But wait a minute, who saved everybody's ass from the Germans in World War I and II, the white power establishments in England and America - RIGHT.

Germanic tribes! That's the original Celts. Hold everything, the earliest known home of the Celts was Germany, wasn't it? WRONG!

Have you heard of CELTIBERIA? Where? Are you ready for this one? SPAIN. The Celts are Spanish or are the Spanish, Celts? Could they be Basques, Moors, Tartars, Arabs, or Africans?

The original Brits were short and long headed, about 5' 5" in height. They spoke a derivative of Celtic and were dark skinned, most likely a distant kin to the Eskimos or African NEGROES! And the Irish will love this one. Who were the FIRBLOGS? Anthropologists tell us they were more pronouncedly NEGROID than even the BRITS. Skeleton structures and ancient descriptions of these natives of the British Isles are still available in England.

The three races were intermixed to create the genetic framework of modern Europe. Unfortunately, due to the lousy PR job done by the NAZIS, ARYANS were alternately referred to as TEUTONS and in turn this became synonymous with Germans. Illogic is necessary to somehow connect white Anglo-Saxons to this nonsense.

Now who is really to blame for the oppression of FEMINISTS, blacks and Hispanics? When in truth, there are no Anglo-Saxons and everybody is everybody else's ancestor.

The ARYAN RACE - no such thing. Interestingly enough, the Aryan culture, civilization and national origins have been traced all the way back to, of all people, the BRAHMINS of INDIA! The Aryan line of descendancy is from Brahmins, to Persians, to Greeks, to Romans, to Teutons. Aryans are originally from the central highlands of ASIA!

In support of what is obviously a complete eradication of RACE as a matter of pride or discrimination is the following set of data extracted from the "Statistical Abstract of the United States, 1984" published by the U. S. Department of Commerce.

The information regarding RACE and Nationalities was compiled from the 1980 census. For simplicity, the numbers have been rounded to the nearest million, and because of their relatively small numbers Chinese, Japanese, Vietnamese, Koreans, etc., I have grouped them together under the title Asian, even though the government insists on designating them as races.

BY RACE

U. S. Total	White	Black	Spanish*	<u>Amer. Indian</u>	Asian	Other
226	188	26	14	**<u>1</u>**	2.9	7

<u>BY NATIONALITY</u>

English	50		Dutch	6
German	50		Swedes	4
Irish	40		Norwegians	4
French	12		Russians	3
Italians	12		Afro-Amer.	21
Scots	10		Mexicans	8
Polish	8		Spanish	3

<u>Amer. Indian</u> **7**

The United States Government sure as hell doesn't comprehend the meaning of RACE. There are three races; pure Negroid, Mongoloid and Caucasian; certainly not Spanish, American Indian, Chinese, Japanese, Vietnamese, Korean, or Other! And you think this is misinformation, how about the Bill of Rights, Article XV, Equal Rights for White and Colored Citizens, "1 . . . on account of race, color . . ."

Keep in mind that black is the absence of color while white is the incorporation of all colors.

Don't you just love the asterisk placed in the statistical table by the Census Bureau? When you read it in the table itself, it states,

* "2. Persons of Spanish origin may be of any race." Now what do you do if you are a "white Spaniard" and you discriminate against a "black Spaniard"?

It's obvious what the FEMINISTS do. They blame it on the white Anglo-Saxon male for discriminating against (you're going to love this) both Hispanics (whoever they are) and blacks. Great bunch of deceptive little broads aren't they!

Don't bother to check the U. S. Total under RACE with the individual totals under NATIONALITIES. Somehow approximately 15 million people fell through the cracks of government. No one seemed to care that six million American Indians were displaced somewhere between their RACE and their NATIONALITY; when in fact they are neither a RACE nor a NATIONALITY.

93

American Jews, probably by mistake, are correctly omitted from being categorized either by RACE or NATIONALITY. Think about that one for a while?

It is interesting that most probably Mexicans and Spaniards were incorrectly classified as Spanish under RACE, but correctly identified separately under NATIONALITY. It is Ironic that both Nationalities often yell discrimination, when it was the Spanish who beat the hell out of the Aztecs, ancestors of the Mexicans.

Remember the AZTECS? They offered human sacrifice of lesser tribes' people to the Gods or perhaps just to obtain necessary protein. It was these same lesser tribes that intermarried Aztecs to become known as Mexicans, who in turn went out and murdered the people of other, even smaller tribes.

The greatest dichotomy of all rests, of course, with the American Negro (black?), who for some crazy reason prefers to be classified as African-American.

There is little or nothing in common between Africans and American Negroes (who at best can only be described as those who are more brown in color than white or Mongolian skin pigmentation) unless American Negroes can directly trace their heritage back to a particular African tribe.

An American Negro may be German, Irish, Nigerian, Jamaican, English, Swedish or some other predominantly historically linked Nationality but not African-American. If one wishes to be classified as African-American then such a description is only comparable to other indigenous continental immigrants, European-Americans, Asia-Americans, Australian-Americans, North-Americans, South-Americans and Antarctic-Americans, if there are any. African-Americans include white South Africans who migrated to North America from South Africa.

There is something so abhorrent in the historical record, the last thing American Negro descendants of slaves should wish to be called is African-Americans. Over a 400 to 500 year period the great-great-great grandfathers of those American slaves took turns, depending on which tribes were in ascendancy, of selling each other's children into slavery!

Despite the rhetoric of "ROOTS", Negroes have more in common genetically, at this late date, with designated whites and so-called Hispanics of America then they do indigenous African Tribes.

Hey! Come on! 1492 AD until 2000 AD, that's almost 500 years made available for one hell of a lot of fooling around amongst Portuguese, Spanish, Aztecs, Indian nations, slaves from African nations, Mexicans, Germans, French, English, Irish, Swedes, Russians, Italians, Poles and God only knows who else.

Literally millions of people from many nations slept their way across the North American continent. The history of interracial copulation is genetically imprinted in our walk, the shape of our noses, the size of our limbs and the shape of our faces to mention only a few significant characteristics other than the color shade of one's skin.

A further, interesting footnote to the lie of white Anglo-Saxon male dominance in America is their supposed desire to perpetuate slavery. First, as established earlier, there is no such thing as white Anglo-Saxon males. If by inference you are obliquely making a racist remark about the English, please keep this in mind. Slavery was abolished in America in 1865. Yet in Africa, intra-tribal slavery flourished up until the 1890's!

By 1890, the British had put into place in their African colonies the rudiments of English law, which forbid slavery! Within their colonies, the British ran afoul of the wealthy monarchical tribal systems of Africa and gained the tribes everlasting animosity when the British used armed might attempting to end slavery in Africa. It was the British that forced the African tribes to give up their centuries' old practice of slavery, slave raiding and slave trading!

Paradoxically, having long ago lost their African "ROOTS", the average great-great-great grandchildren of American slaves, live much better and have a much greater degree of freedom in these United States than do any of today's modern African Negroes!

VII. FEMINIST SEXUALITY

The FEMINIST approach to sex as indicated in the Hite Report is at such a crude level of emotionality as to make a truck driver blush!

What do Masters and Johnson know about all this? Dr. Joyce Brothers, did she know something we don't? Sex therapists-today's shrinks?

Let's start with the results of the Hite Report and see where it might lead in telling us about fulfilling the desires of the modern American FEMINIST. The report is less than statistically accurate by all accounts, but appears to be a bona fide attempt to get at the heart of the American female's sexual preferences and state-of-the-art FEMINIST fantasies.

On the surface, the "Hite Report" gives the impression of reinforcing FEMINIST arguments that they wander through a lifetime of sexual deprivation. The typical illogical conclusion thus jumped upon by one and all is that such deprivation is male induced. Are there alternative, and perhaps ulterior, motivational reasons for the graphic horror stories of self-pity, typified in the excerpts to follow?

Although, there is much controversy over the accuracy of the results, it is reasonable to conjecture that Hite's statistics pertaining to the level of dissatisfaction with the marriage bed are actually conservative; as are the amounts of pleasurable masturbation, frustration, and anger evident in the answers to her questionnaires. All of the compiled data contribute to a singularly provocative battle cry of the FEMINIST. The justification for Lesbianism!

Having no prejudice on the mores of others, I am willing to accept the tabulation of results as conservative estimates. Simply because it would appear, from the vociferousness of the majority of the answers, that more private and shy women, whatever their preferences, would be less likely to reply or divulge the intimacies of their sexual fantasies.

What should be analyzed is the vehemence of the responses indicating very deep emotional shortcomings. Knowledgeable males understand the horrible little confessions hidden within the selfish outrage of supposed failing male sexual performance.

In fact, for those remaining remnants of honest and sensually provocative, American women, I am truly regretful that in your ability to give and receive love, you alone, as women, realize the real hidden results of the report, as opposed to the more popular and politically correct interpretation.

It **wasn't** necessary to select particularly slanted examples from the report to fit the premise of my conclusions. Rather, it was difficult to limit the examples because of the nature of their repetitiveness that depict those areas presenting an overall profile of the "American FEMINIST " in sexual anguish.

Page 130 of the "Hite Report" explicitly delineates the American FEMINIST, lunatic, self-indulgent female mentality.

"I am entitled to orgasms. If I have to masturbate to get them, then my man should also have to masturbate for his and that does not mean masturbating in my vagina . . ."

This American FEMINIST Neanderthal is what the game of FEMINISM and equal rights is really all about. Kindness be damned! Her intellectualized, emotional response speaks crudely but honestly of the true nature of most American FEMINISTS.

A few pages further, the truth coupled with pure garbage.

"Basically I'm too selfish to bother to prove anything to my partners and especially too intelligent to want to do anything to prove I'm a real woman. Bullshit on that!"

Maybe now you will understand what Gloria so innocuously let slip on page 186 of her own book, "Women change the register and language around men." American men simply do not comprehend the other woman in their lives. In many cases it is not the other woman but the multiplicity of actresses within the confines of a single body.

It is any wonder that the American male is so conditioned by the call of the siren, her plaintiff cries for attention create subconscious automatic responses of protectiveness for the "helpless female" or utter frustration with demands couched in coquettish flirtatiousness.

The abilities of the Bene Gesserits of Frank Herbert's great novel, "Dune" are much closer to the truth than might otherwise be suspected.

Of course, there are the responses that more typically identify the hammer in a velvet glove, gentle young FEMINIST maiden of your mythical, take-home-to-mother, girl of your dreams; a real turn on.

"I prefer no sex to bad sex, which to me means sex with a fumbler or a male chauvinist pig, who doesn't let me have an orgasm."

An apt description of an otherwise kind, lovable little woman, wouldn't you agree?

The level of sexual sophistication, experience, emotional stability and intellect of the American FEMINIST is typified by this next eloquent expression of fantasized remembrance:

"No sexual experience has probably ever quite equaled those old high school days in the back seat of a parked car."

The big lie is perpetuated by Hite and further hysterically imprinted upon everyone's data banks by her utilization of references to the old sex therapy groupies, Masters and Johnson.

Hite combines the two great disciplines of asking questions and interpretative observations to reinforce a vaunted female appetite for sex.

"It is widely accepted in sex research that women can have many orgasms in a brief period of time . . ."

She follows this off-the-wall generality by a substantiating, authoritative, Masters and Johnson statement on page 164:

"As contrasted with the male's usual inability to have more than one orgasm in a short period, many females, especially when clitorally stimulated, can regularly have five or six full orgasms within a matter of minutes."

These ludicrous generalizations are, on the whole, gross exaggerations; if not actual incorrect observations and erroneous interpretations based upon typically western type controlled experimental data. As usual, such results are completely isolated from every day reality of American cultural relationships.

If any FEMINIST disbelieves her own insufficiencies, she can, as anyone else, immediately test the relevant truth or fallaciousness of such idiotic generalizations. Such data disassociated from sensuality wrecks havoc on millions of lives, American lives, especially American FEMINIST lives that are totally dependent upon "Expert" advice for everything!

Now all together FEMINISTS, unzip, slither down and on the count of three, begin! Be certain to count and keep track of the clock. For confirmation, consult your friends or better still get 'em all together, right after a hard day at the office and have a multiple launch! Ah, you say, it doesn't work that way, and you are absolutely right. But then Hite quotes Dr. Mary Jane Sharfey:

"The popular idea that a woman should have one intense orgasm that should bring 'full satisfaction', acts as a strong sedative, and alleviates sexual tension for several days to come is simply fallacious."

It simply never occurred to any of these "Sex Experts" that there are at least five other reasons that the conclusion drawn from their interviews and observations are completely fallacious!

- Women lie to satisfy their own fantasy desires. Few if any test subjects in a sexual study environment are going to admit they are not highly sexually stimulated.
- Women have learned to be geniuses at faking orgasms to please their husbands so why not their test clinicians.

- It is more than likely that so called multiple orgasms are simply delightful nerve arousals that when reinforced by fantasy can create the impression that one is having what they, themselves, might consider multiple full-blown orgasms. Knowledgeable, individual real women who have had fully satisfying orgasms know the difference and enjoy both.
- FEMINISTS always blame others for their own lack of arousal.

Meanwhile back at the ranch, the fillies are in heat, confirming the fantasy of every American FEMINIST, page 169:

"I feel like I want twenty . . ."

For the next fifty or more pages, the girls complain, wonder and count their perceived orgasmic explosions! We are then treated to some more "true confessions". Page 227 summarizes the lies that just might also pervade the "controlled experimental data" as well.

"I faked orgasms continuously throughout my marriage . . ."

Thus in modern metaphor, this writer restates the genius of perception in Escher's anomaly:

Which pipe is the real pipe?"

Unlike American FEMINISTS, Escher's pipe had no need for self-discovery.

The modern day FEMINIST graphically illustrates the utter frustration which has become the stock and trade of the American FEMINIST in her never ending search for effortless happiness in the arena of sexual activity. Unknowingly, the Hite Report reveals the hidden frustrated, animal nature of American FEMINISTS. These are women who are unable to have positive giving relationships with members of the opposite sex because of the American FEMINIST need for a living Messiah in all things.

Tabulated results of Hite's inquisitiveness reveal that regardless of statistical accuracy, the overwhelming vindictiveness of FEMINIST responses leave no doubt that a majority of them do not experience orgasm regularly as a result of intercourse.

THE CONSPIRATORIAL NATURE OF THE EVER THEATRICAL, AMERICAN FEMINIST MANIFESTS ITSELF PRIMARILY IN A MARRIAGE BED FARCE.

From a FEMINIST point of view, the ridiculously simple conclusion is to suggest male dominance is tantamount to forcible rape, as can be seen on page 267.

"Insisting women have orgasms during intercourse, is to force women to adapt their bodies to inadequate stimulation."

Arguments to support the male induced frustration of American FEMINISTS are dredged up from old Kinsey studies depicting an either/or answer to their dilemma:

A.   Women can masturbate to orgasm in four minutes.
B.   Only very bodily active women, who jerked and thrusted their clitoris and created a pulling effect on their labia minora experienced satisfactory orgasm during intercourse.

From such Yin-Yang, dipole choices of sexual gratification, the Hite Report reaches an all too obvious media hyped solution; except for various social and religious taboos many more women might be interested in sex with another woman.

The Hite Report's questionnaire studied and tabulated results concerning the sexual needs of the American Woman are best sanctified within the context of the "DONAHUE DOCTRINE".

AMERICAN MEN MUST BE SENSITIVE TO THE NEEDS AND SEXUAL DESIRES MOST GRATIFYING TO AMERICAN WOMEN OR WOMEN WILL SEEK FULFILLMENT IN THE ARMS AND COMFORT OF OTHER WOMEN.

There is, or course, its antithesis:

THE ULTIMATE PERSONIFICATION OF THE RAVENOUSLY RAVAGED, AMERICAN FEMINIST'S MASCULINIZED, SLUT-VIRGIN DICHOTOMY WILL CULMINATE IN RANDY, RAUCOUSLY RAUNCHY, EMOTIONALLY SUICIDAL, FEMINIST CANNIBALISM!

VIII. GRANDMA'S RECEIPT FOR DOING THE FAMILY LAUNDRY!

(Author unknown)

1. Bild a fire in back yard to heet the kettle of rainwater.
2. Set tub so smoke win't blow in eyes if the wind is pert.
3. Shave one hole cake lie soap in biling water.
4. Sort things, make three piles, 1 white pile, 1 pile cullords, 1 pile work britches and rags.
5. Stur foour in cold water to smooth, then thin down with biling water.
6. Rub dirty spots on board, scrubbard, then bile - just rench and starch.
7. Take white things out of kettle with broom handle, then rench, blew and starch.
8. Spred tee towels on grass.
9. Hang old rags on fence.
10. Pore rench water on flowerbeds.
11. Scrub porch with hot soapy water.
12. Turn tubs upsode down.
13. Go put on clean dress - smooth hair with sidecombs - brew cup of tee set and rest and rock a spell and **count your blessings!**

IX. THE GOLDEN PATH
TO FEMININIST GARBAGE

FEMINIST leaders are classic examples of sterile revolutionaries. The most grievous harm pretenders-to-knowledge can inflict is to lead revolutions against the status quo. Too late, their foot soldiers learn that their newly worshipped demigods are vicious slanderers and purveyors of outright lies and half-truths.

Not only does the end not justify the means, but that the results are significantly more grotesque than the previous status quo! For this very reason, the human race has been chewing on its own tail for, at least, the last 5,000 years of recorded history.

The carnage discombobulation created is always referred to as PROGRESS. Let's not muddy the waters of ignorance in the flowing river of greed by learning from past mistakes. Heaven forbid, one might develop a capacity to think. In the words of the often-admired revolutionary hero, Fidel, "What matters is the glory of the leaders, who are all wise because the media says they are!"

American FEMINISTS, ever in search of their fantasy world, continually leap idiotically into intellectual nightmares of sophistry for themselves, their daughters, granddaughters and yet unborn female progeny.

ABORTION

FEMINISTS never ask or answer the really tough questions. If a woman is enamored with the FEMINIST'S movement, and **if she believes it is <u>her decision alone</u> whether or not to have the baby**, then according to her FEMINIST beliefs, the unborn child is hers to do with as she pleases. If she does abort then associated expenses of the operation and ancillary physical, emotional and psychological repercussions are of her own making.

Since the man is excluded from her decision making process, then if the FEMINIST chooses to have the child, she alone is responsible for all costs, care and education of the child.

For DC only FEMINIST lesbians, that choice of course doesn't exist. Why then are they so anxious to give encouragement to others not of the same persuasion in total disregard of their faith?

What are nice Jewish FEMINISTS doing advising Catholic women to abort their children and thus create psychological neurosis concerning the resting place of their immortal souls?

There is another major concern that the FEMINISTS don't acknowledge. Who is going to be around to pick up the pieces of those women's lives that later become filled with guilt and biological revulsion if the FEMINISTS' view is incorrect? But then, long range planning has never been the strong suit of FEMINISTS when faced with instant self-gratification.

By now the Jewish FEMINISTS should really be steaming. The Catholic FEMINISTS mad as hell for reminding them of what they know only too well. Obvious conclusion, I must be a Protestant or at least partial to their beliefs. Wrong again. These FEMINISTS live in the greatest of all conflicting fantasy worlds; by their love of Jesus they are saved, through allowable weaknesses of the flesh they can sin and do as they damn well please.

After all, they believe Jesus is the Son of God, therefore they are saved. Have I missed offending anyone? How about Non-Believer FEMINISTS? They need not share in the hypocrisy of the others, but if they are wrong they are really in for a hot time.

The real story of abortion rights legislation in America can be found in the book, **"Aborting America"** by Bernard N. Nathanson M. D., one of the founders of **NARAL**, **N**ational **A**bortion **R**ights **A**ction **L**eague. For anyone, Right to Life or Freedom of Choice Advocate, who actually consider themselves capable of independent thinking, his book is a must read. If you are afraid of the truth simply don't read it.

Here are some excerpts from his book. Incidentally both Right-To-Lifers and Choice advocates hate his guts for very different reasons.

His is the real story of the history and tragedy of the Abortion Rights Movement. Here are a few excerpts.

From February of 1971 until September of 1972 he was the Director of the Center for Reproductive and Sexual Freedom. The center was the largest and busiest abortion clinic in the world. Nathanson was also Chief of Obstetrical Services at St. Luke's Hospital in New York City. In his book, Nathanson stated, that by 1974 he had ". . . in fact presided over 60,000 deaths" (Abortions!).

On page 32, Nathanson speaks about a man named Lawrence Lader who was educated at prep school and a Harvard graduate who published a book titled, "Abortion". Larry came from a New York family of considerable means. He was interested in radical politics and revolutionary thinking. In the early 1940's he worked for Vito Marcontonio, N.Y. congressman so leftist in his opinion he was widely suspected of being a communist.

Nathanson quotes Larry as having said, "Well Bernie you know what Margaret always said 'no woman can call herself free who does not own and control her body'". Nathanson goes on to say, " I knew of his 1955 biography of Margaret Sanger and that he still worshipped the birth-control crusader, but his use of her first name in so familiar a manner jarred me a little."

"Remarkably **Margaret Sanger** had always **opposed abortion**." Again on page 32, "Betty Freidan had organized NOW the year before and was at that time already contenting with dissension in its ranks from the Trotskyite left, the lesbian libbers and the more rabid pro-abortionists."

On page 33, Larry brought out his favorite whipping boy, ". . . and the other thing we're got to do is bring Catholic hierarchy out where we can fight them; that's the real enemy. The biggest single obstacle to peace and decency throughout all of history."

On page 36 we learn that Larry is also a founder of NARAL.

On page 182, "Strange the Right-to-Lifers do not make more of the fact that the pioneer in liberal abortion was not Hitler but V. Lenin in 1920. The Soviet Union is not exactly one's ideal of humanitarianism, life valuing state, either."

On page 193, "How many deaths were we talking about when abortion was illegal? In N.A.R.A.L. we generally emphasized the drama of the individual case, not the small statistics, but when we spoke of the latter it was always **5,000 to 10,000 deaths a year."**

"I confess that I knew the figures were totally false . . . but in the 'morality' of our revolution, it was a useful figure, widely accepted. Statistics on abortion deaths were fairly reliable, since bodies are difficult to hide . . . **in 1967 . . . the Federal Government listed only 160 deaths from illegal abortion . . . 1972, the total was only 39 deaths . . . the actual total was probably closer to 500."**

"The death of 500 women, or even 39, is a matter of the most serious concern, but this is hardly an overwhelming death rate among millions of women in childbearing age . . . it might be lopsided for a society to consider only 500 women and ignore the 1,000,000 alphas that are legally extinguished each year."

Alphas are FEMINIST euphemisms for aborted babies.

On pages 248-249, "There are 75,000 abortions in my past medical career . . . and 1,500 I performed myself . . . I now regret this loss of life. I thought the abortions were right at the time; revolutionary ethics are often unrecognizable at some future, more serene date. The errors of history are not recoverable; the lives cannot be retrieved. One can only pledge to adhere to an ethical course of action in the future."

Throughout his book, Nathanson **reveals the lies and deceptions used to gain American FEMINISTS the right to legalized Abortions.**

Who really manipulates whom in this never-ending battle between the sexes? Enjoyment, fantasy, long life, happiness and infinite masturbation of mind and body belong rightfully to American FEMINISTS because they suffer in childbirth! Go get em gals, straight to the heart, marry em, give em a little flesh, and then plead misunderstanding and involuntary slavery.

From time to time send them off to war and then start in all over again. Meanwhile, the dumb guys dig the coal, build the skyscrapers, fix the plumbing and dutifully go off and die for you. Gosh, I just remembered, there are a couple of FEMINIST coal miners and, OH! that beauty in Flashdance, now there is your typical American FEMINIST. Right girls?

EQUAL PAY FOR EQUAL WORK - a great rally cry of injustice. How does that song and dance go for public support and the talk show hosts? Women only average about 70% of the average weekly wage of the white American male. Notice how conveniently is omitted the black American male.

"A recent survey of workers proves that . . . blah, blah, blah . . . therefore American FEMINIST are entitled to . . ." The missing word is always the same . . . MORE! There are many more small details the feminists leave out of their "facts".

Let's not allow the truth to get in the way of more self-gratification. One of the major reasons the average wage difference between men and women exists is due to the higher wages of men in the skilled trades. Not necessarily high enough to compensate for their real contribution to the easy life of most Americans.

Their working conditions are difficult, dirty and often times dangerous. These men create the tools, machines and power grids by which the terribly underpaid, poor little American FEMINISTS have the opportunity to buy everything their little hearts desire.

These men, the backbone of American industry, work, not because it's a nice way to spend the day. Men perform these back-breaking labors because they want to see that their families get the best the sweat of their minds and bodies can buy.

The skilled trades in America are actually <u>vastly underpaid professions</u>! But because harebrained educators placed such a high priestess, false image on college degrees, the skilled tradesmen are the real under privileged class in America when compared to the output of the average working American FEMINIST. To become a skilled tradesman requires a high degree of special skills and a number of apprenticeship years.

It is the wages of these very skilled professionals skewing the averages in favor of males; professions such as tool and die makers, machinists, steamfitters, plumbers, carpenters, and electricians. The list is endless and a few hardy women are included in the millions of everyday males who hold these very difficult jobs that American FEMINISTS are just dying to fill; not to mention the plain hard, backbreaking labor of plasterers, hod carriers, and steelworkers.

All that's required is that you work sometimes 12 hour days in heat exceeding 110° F, in dirty, dangerous, and toxic environments; requiring great physical effort, extensive knowledge of math, how to read blueprints and use of precision tools under constant stress.

If a truly fair scale of comparable work were devised, then by comparison FEMINIST wages on the average would fall far below what they presently earn in relation to the average male. Come on libbers, let's climb those 600 foot steel towers and string those electric wires in high rises and carry 80 pounds of wet plaster up the ladders on your strong little backs.

Meanwhile, you can relax. Breathe in those carbon dust fumes while dangling your toes over the edge of steel girders for lunch break. Enjoy the sound of 150 decibel air hammers ringing in your ears or listen to the melodic piped in music of a drop forge all day long, until you finally drop from all manner of industrial diseases.

Yes, thousands of women do perform some of these tasks, but ladies we are talking about millions of men spending 40 to 50 years of their lives at these labors. And some dumb FEMINIST broad gets on a talk show and complains, and complains, and complains.

For relaxation the guy gets to come home and listen to what a rough day the little FEMINIST put in. How little Johnny is driving her crazy, and what she needs is to become a doctor, lawyer, social worker, or magazine editor to reach her life fulfillment goals in her air conditioned office, high above the riffraff in the Big Apple.

No more little enslaved housewives. No siree, now it's little old enslaved "Career" women. Just how much does it take to satisfy your lust for the unobtainable, as if we didn't know, EVERYTHING!

ERA - the term if correctly understood, means that when someone is good at something then there should exist the legal right to compete and be judged on one's merit for the position. Say for example, a girl is good enough to play on a boy's basketball team. She should be able to get the position based on merit.

Wait a minute! What about the thousands of boys who are much more superior athletes than the girls on girls' teams? Shouldn't boys be given the opportunity to play instead of the girls? Oh! I see! If there were such a thing as a true ERA, then all the teams would be made up of mostly boys, but somewhere there is an obvious paradox.

What about the boys' rights, their lost opportunities? What about their unfulfilled lives? Obviously boys in all level of athletics are discriminated against in favor of privileged girls. All court cases are tried on behalf of the exceptional female athlete.

What about the thousands of boys who could easily outperform her? Shouldn't these more qualified boys be playing on the varsity girls' teams instead of the girls? The top 200 ranked male, pro tennis players can beat Martina and Venus. Some women pros say they can be beaten by the top 1000 male professional tennis players!

Most of 1,000 male pros earn far less than do the top twenty women pros Why is it for the same purses women tennis players only play three sets not five sets as the men often do?

FEMINISTS, what the hell have you to gain from the likes of Friedan and Steinem? I can't quite lump Germaine in with these other two characters who head your lovely "all the sheep to the cliff" club.

Germaine commits the unpardonable sin of, from time to time, falling in love. Her book "The Female Eunuch" on the surface appears logical and is well written. It even makes the plea, heaven forbid, for women to tell the truth.

One should remember that most of the so-called brilliant "NOW" girls come from the Eastern Establishment educational system. These same FEMINISTS, often times with **little or no** real life struggles or experience, actually come to believe what they read and are taught on the laps of their mentors, male and female professors. Whatever the excuses, these so-called intellectuals never had an original, let alone an unselfish thought in their entire lives.

X. ROCK, MARX, FREUD & PROHIBITION

The frivolously constructed environment of American FEMINISTS leaves them highly susceptible to every crackpot notion placed before the poisoned banquet table of humanity. American FEMINISTS, and they alone, from their position of world dominance, perpetuate and enshrine more idiotic activities than the remainder of the human race combined.

Why Americans FEMINISTS and not other women? And, of course, the really nagging question at this stage of confrontation, what about men? Well girls, you're not going to like the answer. It just so happens that you and you alone obtained the heights of comparative world richness and luxury! Time and well being, two of the most important ingredients for shaping world events, coupled with the most responsible assignment incumbent upon any member of the human race, were yours for the taking.

The care and nurturing of the next generation of human beings is the most gratifying and important responsibility of any society. The fundamental thesis underlying all that follows in cataloging the irresponsibility of FEMINISTS hinges on those indisputable facts.

No other group in recorded history has had more labor saving conveniences, leisure time (PRE-FEMINISM), a greater opportunity for higher education, while at the same time, little or no responsibility over prolonged periods of their lifetime.

Was this time spent in the pursuit of wisdom and knowledge and the betterment of their fellow human beings? Or was it spent wastefully on their daydreams and fantasies in pursuit of selfishness? Ah! One can hear the anguished cries throughout the land. How dare he? Male chauvinist pig! Right Wing Fascist!

On and on drones the tired FEMINIST rhetoric in an attempt at misdirection. All kinds of invectives, self-justifications, superfluous arguments, and extraneous subject matter will be introduced in counter argument to turn the reader's head aside from the simple truth of this book. Truth from which there is no escape.

The children of America were led to believe that their fathers were constantly out drinking, having a great time and chasing skirts. In their spare time those same maligned men just happened to have worked their asses off creating the most affluent society to date upon the face of this earth.

Indictment of failure cannot be laid at the doorstep of those who might have been responsible for the youth of the country. No girls, the failures rest solely with those who were responsible. The record of the FEMINISTS monumental failure is a result of complete ineptitude.

We are not discoursing on some hypothetical situation or some short term, misguided, irresponsible behavior. No indeed, we are speaking about wholesale incompetence since the beginning of this new wave of FEMINISTS. There are exceptions and FEMINISTS will waste no time in dredging them up. They are exceedingly adept at producing exceptions to the rule representing the case for the majority. Therefore, before citing chapter and verse, it is necessary to diffuse their usual scurrilous ploys by stating the obvious.

<u>THERE ARE TENS OF MILLIONS OF WOMEN IN AMERICA WHO DO NOT DESERVE TO BE PLACED IN THIS WRETCHED CATEGORY OF FEMINISTS.</u>

One of the purposes of this book is to erase from the minds of its readers all the claptrap that has been heaped on the heads of the White Anglo-Saxon males by FEMINISTS and the empty headed news media, such as:

A. WOMEN ARE GENETICALLY SUPERIOR TO MEN AND THEREFORE LIVE LONGER.

Women in America live longer because on the whole they have led healthier and more comfortable lives with less stress and more leisure-time (PRE-FEMINISM). If, in fact, women really equally share the difficult lifetime hard work of the average American male, women too will have shorter life spans.

B. WOMEN ARE TIED TO A LIFE OF DRUDGERY RAISING A HOUSEFUL OF KIDS.

FEMINISTS have so constructed their lives as to give that impression for the purpose of creating a sense of guilt within their husbands. Men then become more susceptible to the whims and fantasies of these women.

The majority of American families have two children or less. Statistically this means that some families have more than two. Except for the first five years of a child's life, it is difficult to imagine any halfway-organized individual spending more than four hours a day taking care of wifely responsibilities for two children and a husband.

If baby raising years for two children are maximized at ten, for the remaining 13 years (youngest child would then be 18) the majority of American Women could comfortably (physically and psychologically) devote four hours a day caring for the family. Then if married at or before 21 years of age, the majority of women would be almost completely free of any family responsibility <u>by the age of forty-four</u> (10 + 13 + 21) (PRE-FEMINISM).

C. WOMEN ARE UNDERPAID IN THE AMERICAN WORK FORCE.

It is true that for many years women have been protected by labor laws from the more rigorous toils of the labor force in such areas as the number of hours worked per week and the amount of physical weight to be lifted. Yes FEMINISTS, we are aware of sewing machine sweatshops and similar exceptions to the rule. Again, I must remind you we are speaking about the norm that is unless you wish to include comparison to ironworkers, sewer cleaners, and trash collectors.

D.   WOMEN ARE ROMANTIC AND LOVING. MEN ARE PRAGMATIC AND SELFISH.

In actual practice FEMINISTS are very pragmatic and hardheaded. Their early primary objective is to get out from under the authority of their own mothers. It is their mothers who know them only too well, and who have been in mutual, combatant, biological warfare with their daughters over control of the father for years.

From the outset of puberty and thereafter, a non-lesbian FEMINIST sets out to find herself an idealized mate. When all else fails, she decides upon a career. Nowadays, she decides upon a career because she actually believes what she is told about self-fulfillment or surmises it is a better means of finding the idealized mate.

The quickest means to success is by offering her body to seek protection; whatever it takes to gain security and dominance.

Security and well being that elude her because fantasy is her greatest enemy. It is this unrelenting fantasy world that creates enormous problems for the remainder of her life. Her ever-present needs are always uppermost in her mind. Deceptions to fulfill those needs start very early in her life. Because of her self-deluding fantasies, she is absolutely bubble headed when it comes to the core workings of her life. Always avoiding the real world, the American FEMINIST immerses herself in a world of fantasy!

It is this fantasy world which we shall explore and point out the devastating effects it has on the social fabric of America. Because of the very nature of American FEMINISTS there is no need for chronological order or a logical approach to the subject matter. The consequences of an American FEMINIST'S individual actions appear frivolous enough; however, in concert her fantasies lay the groundwork for all that wrecks havoc on today's world!

Rock, Marx, Freud and Prohibition say more about the mental aberrations of American FEMINISTS than all the obligatory rhetoric which can be thrown on the outhouses of these women's tormented lives for the remainder of this intellectual discombobulation. Gods and their representatives hold a singular fascination, as bodily removed, effusive, sexual, fantasy images for carnivorous young and old FEMINISTS; be they Valley, Virgin, Slut or All American!

<u>ROCK</u>

Rock, Rap and Pop stars and their music epitomize the general sense of adoration, without obligation, that FEMINISTS teenage girls and their FEMINISTS mothers can drool over in unison. It is whimsical idolatry that is not separated by ethnic, social or monetary boundaries. Much like male movie stars, the plastic music idols fall heir, or is it prey, to the FEMINIST mess of neurotic girls and future mothers. The smart idols take the money and the gratuitous sex as part and parcel of the business. Those idols that succumb to their media images are simply relegated to the trash heap of trivia.

Should the rockers be so unfortunate as to sleep with one or more of these miserable whining creatures, the "Idol" will quickly learn that these girls are not the cream of the crop. Rather, the idol of the day, the legend of his time, finds himself saddled with teeny-boppers who believe they are really in love.

The teenybopper's more intelligent peers should remind her, "Honestly sweetheart, you can scream for their love from the audience, but for God's sake we don't bring them home to mother! That part of our lives is reserved for doctors, lawyers and other professional men who can take care of us."

These already screwed up FEMINISTS, entrenched in their world of fantasy, go on to college. They become bedded puppets of the campus radical political heroes and certain megalomaniacs amongst college FEMINIST inclined professors. Those revolutionary malcontents of every age, who establish the conditions from which emerge a continuous stream of over-educated FEMINISTS. Over-educated is a euphemism for lacking in common sense and moral integrity.

One of the saddest revelations aired many years ago, in a news interview on a major TV network, dealt with another verification of the juvenile, serendipitous, fantasy world lunacy in which American FEMINISTS indulge themselves in deprivation of their own best interest.

In a TV interview, a nephew of Sigmund Freud, Edward Bennal, who became known as the father of public relations on Madison Avenue, spoke about what he and the media believed at the time was a very amusing incident. It seems that just after World War II, the president of a leading tobacco company in America, R .J. Reynolds Co, hired Freud's nephew to find a method whereby more American Women would pick up the habit of smoking, thereby doubling the market for tobacco products. Did the public relations expert engage the services of a brilliant, all male advertising agency to addict American Women to cigarettes?

On national TV was explained the simple manner in which such an enormous injury to the health of a nation was created in just a SINGLE DAY by appealing to the VANITY and ME FIRST attitude of American FEMINISTS.

The public relations expert called a number of his FEMINIST, New York socialite friends, whom he knew championed equal rights for women. He suggested within the context of lengthy phone conversations that, . . . wouldn't it be marvelous if the crème de la crème of New York's FEMINISTS appeared at the forefront of the upcoming Easter Sunday Parade, smoking like chimneys for all the world to see. After all men smoked in public, therefore women, by all means, must have what men have!

The gung-ho FEMINISTS alerted newspapers throughout the country and encouraged by word of mouth that all women in the Easter Parade smoke. Within two weeks, after the New York Easter Parade, smoking in public was the inalienable right of every American Woman!

Congratulations FEMINISTS, not only did you create a lot of jobs for female cigarette advertising models on radio, TV and newspapers, you are solely responsible for the major source of female lung cancer and you created the process of pre-birth nicotine addiction of the youth of America. Another cultural great leap forward!

<u>MARX</u>

Time and again, American FEMINISTS have screwed up. They pass on one nutty notion after another from generation to generation. What you have read so far is only the beginning. Take a peek at a few insights into two of your late, great dummies of the nineteenth and twentieth centuries, Karl Marx and his pragmatic alter ego Lenin!

Remember the movie "REDS", the hero, John Reed, played by Warren Beatty and the heroine played by Diane Keaton, working side by side to save the world from democracy. How idealistic, romantic and thrilling; brotherly love, equal rights for women, paradise for workers, etc.

No, DUMB, REALLY DUMB! In fact, latest revelations from opened KGB files show that Reed, to the tune of 1,000,000 rubles, was in the pay of what later became the KGB.

There is no such thing as Capitalism versus Communism, only different types of people in power who will always take advantage of other people. Like millions of card-carrying members of the Communist party in the Soviet Union who lived very well by their standards by taking from the other 200 million of their countrymen.

Just like the same number of dedicated members on the inside of the Republican and Democratic parties in the United States live very well off the rest of us, except for two major differences:

A. If you argued over there, you got shot!

B. Here, you live one hell of a lot better.

Our system is inhabited by politicians without consciences, but the Communist system was simply ridiculous. Oh! And one other thing, American FEMINISTS just happen to live on the best piece of real estate in this solar system.

Why do I seemingly digress, bringing into focus Communist Russia? Because many of the same ideas instilled in the <u>jerk-water, small town American FEMINIST libbers' minds</u>, spring forth from the bastions of the eastern girl's educational establishment. Where FEMINIST leaders learned from the lap, or more likely the bed, of many, far removed from reality professors. **Small town in this context refers to mainly New York City and the eastern seaboard.** The area of the country where the last good idea came from an Indian. He sold Manhattan Island and headed West, hopefully not to California!

You have read in the first three chapters the verification of all that is written here in the very own words of the modern day founders of the new wave of American FEMINISTS!

The 1917 Bolshevik Revolution began oddly enough back in the 1880's. A group of fifty young Jewish girls and their professors were placed in jail for protesting the policies of Czarist Russia. From this sprang the Russian Bund (Jewish worker and young intellectual organization). Their cause and their methods of operation became the later foundation for the party "cell" structure of the Communist party in its worst aberrational form.

So much for dumb young girls, intellectual conversationalists, Karl Marx and Lenin, believe me, you don't wish to have me relate the complete story of this misguided, frivolous, romantic movement which became a murderous, blood bath nightmare.

True knowledge of the past can be dangerous to your fantasies and to others' interests about which you are meant to know nothing. The pain of facing the truth would make it possible for you to "THINK" for yourselves and that is the last thing American Feminists really desire.

FREUD

Freud, the modern day founder of female neuroses, has Western Civilization, and in particular FEMINISTS hooked on occult belief that makes African tribal witch doctors seem positively Einsteinian by comparison.

Where else but in America can you find millions of people willing to pay $ 100 an hour so that FEMINISTS (and any with equally nutty spouses) can have another, just as screwed up individual listen to their self-serving confessions, my problems, my mental illness, my dreams, my childhood . . . my, my, my . . . my, my! The solution to their dilemma is self-evident.

If Sigmund Freud with all his own psychotic hang-ups hadn't happened, modern American medicine would have had to create him. Why? Because medical doctors have been driven crazy by complaining FEMINISTS. Finally, for self-protection, the doctors refer them to that special branch of modern medicine and prosper while the girls are nicely treated and their neuroses are confirmed.

FEMINISTS who don't get professional help shouldn't become smug. You know, don't you dears, that if you had the right medical plan, social worker or sugar daddy you too would be ME-OWING!

Sigmund Freud, the intellectual giant, left another tainted gift of his genius to western civilization, COCAINE. He idolized the junk, was hooked on it, and recommended it to the world as mankind's greatest cure for everything.

Oh! And what about his celebrated couch? Freud was too inhibited to listen to the fantasies and complaints of his female patients eyeball to eyeball. To avoid direct eye contact he had them lie prone on a couch. Somebody should have administered a Rorschach test to Sigmund before things got out of hand.

PROHIBITION

It's all yours, sweethearts, the whole bit. Let's see that makes some more of your well thought out FEMINIST'S idealisms unable to stand the test of time or sensibility. You financed the Mafia, created an entire nation of alcoholics and put JFK in office (that one will require some real detective work). Of course, the entire idea went hand in hand with the suffragette movement giving women the right to vote, which would enlighten all mankind as to the political brilliance of FEMINIST intuition!

With such enlightened FEMINISM, America became embroiled in World War II, the Korean, Vietnam and Gulf wars. The illogic of FEMINIST, time worn self-justification to become little men rather than glorious women has created a nightmare in human relations from which the world may neither have the time or the inclination to recover.

American FEMINISTS are totally fantasy driven, selfish, conniving and traitorous to those to whom they owe everything, including love, <u>THEMSELVES</u>! They are their own worst enemies.

Now just who the hell are the Steinems, the Greers and the Friedans and their nefarious compatriots; those stellar intellectuals who have lead the poor dumb sheep to yet one more slaughter?

What have these three women done in their illustrious lives or, better yet, what have they written, and what life substance credentials have they brought to humanity which entices American FEMINISTS into committing, if nothing else, economic suicide. What is so persuasive in their rhetoric that can lead millions of groupies, like a bunch of dumb bunnies, down the path to yet another misbegotten fantasy?

Do these FEMINIST idols represent in prose what the Rock and Pop stars represent in music - everything American FEMINISTS want without earning it? How many generations are going to screw up before sitting down and learning about the realities of life? Have any FEMINIST actually read from cover to cover even one of their founders' kooky books, let alone two or heaven forbids, perhaps all three?

XI. THE GREAT FEMINIST DILEMMA

This is a problem in pure logic without any emotional component. If you are a FEMINIST can you function logically?

Those practicing abortion, due to unwanted pregnancies, have **<u>serious problems</u>** in the long run. Of course, they **avoid** the failure associated with practicing the Art of Parental Love, as well as the discomfort associated with pregnancy and birthing as well as the possibility of not being loved in turn by a child.

Over-population is a concern of everyone. Abortion by false personalities is not a very satisfactory solution to the problem. Common sense birth control, through contraception, is a much more planned approach to the problem. Of course, avoiding unprotected sex and choosing the right husband go without saying.

Abortion, almost without exception, is due to accidental and unplanned sexual activity in which the individuals have little, if any, forethought or real concern about population control.

Those practicing and advocating abortion have taken on a very difficult, long-term responsibility that they, themselves, do not comprehend or they choose to ignore at the time of the abortion.

Their false personalities, filled with the fear of the pregnancy, as well as social and financial concerns, are intent upon only short-term objectives and easy solutions to their immediate indiscretion. Individuals, who have multi-abortions, are truly disturbed false personalities and are immediate self-gratification addicts.

Those caught up in a one-time situation, face (excluding the real possible danger of the abortion procedure, itself) serious long-term, psychological problems, long-term physical health problems and the real possibility they cannot procreate at some future time.

The human body is not very tolerant in the long run of medical practices that drastically interrupt natural, healthy, human life, bodily function activities.

The psychological repercussions of pro-choice advocates are beyond measure should one change one's mind with regard to their religious belief system later in life, not to mention hormonal, biological repercussions and possible later life loneliness.

Everyone needs to be very certain of their religious belief system as one deviates from celibacy in regard to sexual matters.

The ramifications depending upon one's belief system, if based upon the directive, "Thou shalt not kill" carry eternal consequences in regard to practicing or advocating abortion.

Any individual advocating or practicing abortion and claims to be of the Jewish, Muslim or Christian faith is at best an irrational human being; or at worst a heinous hypocrite. Heinous because there is a fifty-fifty chance, one is advocating murder in violation of the fifth commandment of their supposed religious belief.

Don't confuse such a fact as based upon belief but rather it is based upon pure logic. If you are a member of one of these religions then by choice you believe in the Ten Commandments as the Word of God. But such an individual will argue that he or she doesn't believe that a fetus should be classified, as a human being; therefore the embryo is not protected by that Commandment.

But **no one really knows** if the previous statement is true. Therefore there is at least a 50% chance that the embryo in the eyes of their God is protected by the Fifth Commandment. Only a heinous hypocrite or an irrational person would gamble eternity in hell on a fifty percent chance of guessing correctly!

XII. YOU'VE COME A LONG WAY BABY!

From prohibition to hard rock via Karl Marx and Sigmund Freud, ignoring grandma's sage advice, dancing on the brink of madness and total chaos, yes indeed FEMINISTS, you've come a long way baby! Lacking in true self-confidence, that is built upon the rigors of conscious labor and intentional suffering, you live in a make believe world of fantasy, utterly selfish and self-centered.

American males have no comprehension of women in general, let alone "American FEMINIST Women". Therefore, the men are completely helpless in regard to assisting you out of the quagmire of multiple dilemmas into which you have gleefully chosen to cast yourselves.

The statistical compilation of the disasters of your sheep-to-the-cliffs psychological, mass suicidal mentality is mounting faster than the "experts" can create new speculations for the causes:

- 25% of American children (14 million) are below the poverty line.
- The major cause is female led, single households.

- 70% of married women work compared to 5% in 1900.
- Pregnancy among unmarried girls is epidemic.
- One million abortions annually in the United States.
- SAT scores (when not doctored) at an all time low.
- Literacy in the inner cities is under 50%.
- Large city high school drop out rates above 40% 400,000 annually attempted, reported teenage suicides
- Female lung cancer rate astronomically accelerating.
- Biological clocks running out on modern
- FEMINISTS.
- Vast numbers of more aggressive young FEMINISTS snapping at your heels.
- Sheer panic settling into your unmarried, old age bones.
- Unmarried women, fastest growing poverty-stricken Group.
- Women, not men, your major competition
- Men, no longer married while still immature are not susceptible to trading marriage, room and board for sex metered out between headaches.

FEMINISTS, you have been swindled out of your very lives by those who would cater to your greedy, underdeveloped masculine personality traits at the expense of sacrificing your most precious possession, your feminine natures. Everyday, you paste on your Max Factor faces and go forth to emulate the inane, stupid, nonsensical objectives of the Betty Friedans and Gloria Steinems of this world.

"NOW" instead of being trapped by the "Feminine Mystique" you are willing slaves of the "Career Mystique"! And what does your fearless old leader Friedan have to say about the great revolution and its progress?

After over fifty years of utter disaster by her own chosen standards, Old Betty thinks there has been a few small mistakes, but all in all the entire grand screw up of your lives has been a marvelous success.

Previously, you baffled young, immature males into believing that they were poor lovers and uncaring husbands, with your coquettishness and Victorian morals; baited with unspoken promises of sexual bliss for which you received free room and board. The poor saps actually believed you loved them. Never realizing you settled for what you could get and fantasized the rest.

American men thought love, honor and obey were promises you made. They never dreamed you meant men should love you, honor your every whim and fulfill your every wish gratification. Meanwhile, you went on dreaming, all day long, about your lost love or the Prince Charming you so richly deserved.

You drove the poor bastards to providing more and more and more, until there simply was no more and then you became bored. Along came Betty and her great alter ego, Sarah. The country as a whole rallied to your demands, tens of millions of jobs were literally created out of thin air. "NOW" comes the hard part.

The jobs are not "Careers". They are just plain old jobs. The same old jobs most American men have gone to day after day all their lives. No time to enjoy their families, indulge in daydreaming or become bored in their nine room concentration camps.

Masculine ears have turned stone deaf to your constant complaining and self-serving arguments. Frankly, my dears nobody gives a damn! Despite the rhetoric of "NOW", men work because they were groomed for generation upon generation by their mothers, grandmothers, their mothers and mothers before them. These men dedicated their lives to create an enormously wealthy society for self-indulgent FEMINISTS.

95%, perhaps 98%, of American men never had "Careers".

They had and still have just plain old jobs which everyday they come home from, looking for a little love, care and attention, only to find whining, complaining, self-centered "over-worked" FEMINIST harpies. American men have been raised to believe their task in life was to spend their youth and well into old age providing the best of everything for their families, particularly their wives. Theirs are the lives of lonely men that the FEMINISTS so envy.

So "NOW" girls, it's your turn - have fun, enjoy the next lonely fifty or sixty years. You certainly deserve it! Fantasize your hearts out, dream about the perfect father, provider, lover, husband, handsome doctor, or that understanding, affectionate mate who just can't wait to satisfy your every demand.

The great, fantasized lover of your life expects nothing in return. He will give you everything, the plane, the gas, hold the door, and help you into the plane, turn it into the wind and waits with bated breath while you declare you owe everything to yourself and fly off into the sunset to a glorious "Career".

What about those horrible men who cheat on their wives? Who is the willing partner to such dastardly deeds if not one of your "Sisters?" Come on FEMINISTS, the jig is up! You know each other only too well. Each of you would steal any man from any other woman if you could. Sisterhood, shmisterhood! You're the greatest biological huntresses of all time. The mere scent of an ideal mate and your little devious minds concoct all manners of fanciful scenarios!

Sure the work-a-day world is a nice place in which to play, but no one in her right mind wants to live there.

On the other hand, if your lesbian relationship isn't spawned from fear of childbirth and the possibility of accepting responsibility, good luck upon entering a relationship with someone that thinks exactly as you do. You deserve each other. Please girls, spare us the one in a million example for which FEMINISTS are famous.

If yours is truly the golden path of FEMINIST garbage, then follow the empty headed pretenders to knowledge. Just remember, when you are a basket case of unrequited desires and unfulfilled ambitions, it wasn't the poor guy you spit on for the grand adventure of the "Sarahs" of this world who got you into this mess. All your subsequent greedy little problems and failures are created by yourselves and your verbose, small minded, greedy, little revolutionary leaders.

You are, of course, a great disappointment to the cause. You are the greediest bunch of consumers the world has ever known.

You have flown in the face of your numero uno leader, Betty. You have completely invalidating the major premise of her prognostication, that as college educated, brilliant "Career" FEMINISTS you would topple Madison Avenue and with it destroy the mythical capitalistic base upon which America is constructed. You would thereby set the stage for a marvelous new Communistic Society, ala Betty, Gloria, Fidel and Lenin and Marx!

I'm sorry to say FEMINISTS that you have been such a disappointment that you may be forcibly put back into your nine room concentration camps for screwing up the leader's plans; to say nothing of making a mockery of all her crackpot assumptions.

If all else fails one can always turn to leader dos, Gloria, "great in emergencies, but can't handle everyday life." Steinem. The "NOW" FEMINIST'S model of perfection, a journalist of the highest integrity, is a well spring of authoritative knowledge and wisdom.

She was a sweet little failed actress that blamed her father for her mother's illicit love affair and later "miscarriage". Gloria found her mother's lover, and editor and co-worker . . . more than any man ought to be."

Gloria's "Sisterhood" consists of sleazy little comrades working day and night to wrest POWER from men and saving American FEMINISTS from a fate worse than death, " . . . little murders in our bedrooms and little love."

Her peeping "Gloria sleuthing" failed to correctly identify the real victim! All this from a sly girl who when she couldn't hack it in Toledo went to Smith or vise-versa. Once ensconced in the halls of dear old Smith, little Gloria got an ed . . . u. . . . ca. . . . tion from professor bed sheet, a great intellectual teacher of Econ. 101 or perhaps English Lit. 203.

Lest we forget, Betty Friedan, the foreboding genius of the FEMINIST movement, is a graduate psychologist, the darling of the Smith girls. She actually read "Chaucer" on the green grass lawns of Smith. Because of her fabrication of laying the blame for all America's misfortunes on the "Feminine Mystique", there are now millions of starving women and children in the United States of America, a million abortions annually, rampant sexual diseases and unbridled FEMINIST consumerism.

Friedan claimed all these problems were caused by mothers staying at home. Then why have such problems multiplied to monstrous proportions during the fifty years of the FEMINIST movement?

According to HER OWN DEFINITION, "NOW" is a total failure. Being a fair and impartial researcher, presented with such obvious proof of the absolute refutation of all her theories according to statistical correlation, observation, and just plain common sense, would Betty come forth, as would any honest woman, and recant her earlier stupidity? Would she admit that the era of the "Feminine Mystique" was, by comparison to "NOW", American Women's finest hour?

NO, old hard-nosed Friedan arrogantly tells us that perhaps there were a few minor mistakes. Everything is going according to plan. Her plan is to make every American woman as unhappy and as intellectually dishonest as she is. The FEMINIST movement is a total disaster, an abysmal failure!

Female consumerism is greater than ever. social diseases are almost beyond control. Women are at each other's throats over the question of abortion. Divorce rates are astronomical.

Crime is everywhere you look. FEMINISTS are filling the couches of shrinks by the thousands. The list of failures mounts faster than anyone can imagine. Betty's new social order just goes rolling along creating utter chaos, not for men, for WOMEN!

Dumb old husbands in bygone days were encouraged by shrewder women than the present lot to chase the illusion of great "Careers" in order to satisfy the American FEMINIST'S desire to have everything. That illusion kept men in servitude to their wives and family from early manhood through old age retirement unto death.

FEMINISTS became jealous of their own self-serving created myth. "NOW" the seducers have been themselves seduced; led by crazy mixed up pseudo-intellectuals and the outmoded folklore beliefs in sisterhood, destruction of Capitalism, Communism for the greater good, lesbianism, and powerful "Careers".

We are told that the key to this mythical power is "education", preferably as defined by the liberal arts curriculum of the Eastern Girls' College courses, such as art history, sociology, Econ. 101

and the modern American novel. Sociology and psychology are the dream courses for FEMINISTS who can't even control themselves. It gives them entree and government license to go out and meddle in other people's lives.

These watered down educational curriculums are for simple-minded individuals who love to moon and swoon over the romantic antics and con-artistry of their beautiful professors. These FEMINISTS comprise, on the whole, the most narrow minded bunch of messed up illiterates to ever grace the proverbial green grass lawns of America's "Finest" women's colleges.

Yet in one way or another, a great many American women have bought all or part of the FEMINISTS shoddy "intellectual" wares. Unfortunately, you can't buy a little bit of Communism without getting a whole lot of Joe Stalin and Lenin; anymore than you can buy a little bit of "NOW" without getting the whole enchilada.

Anyone who condemns Nazi Germany while extolling the glories of Communism is simply intellectually and emotionally dishonest. Such individuals, faced with their duplicity, cry discrimination or declare such truth as Fascist propaganda.

FEMINISTS deviously shelter their prevarications beneath the horrible price paid by all European Jews for the dual evil of Communism and Nazism. But people such as Gloria and Betty would have you believe that the Nazis were devils and totally evil. While the Communists, occasionally, are just zealously excessive in their pursuit of the common good.

The really sick part of the whole thing is that for almost one hundred years, and most assuredly for the past seventy years, Americans have been told that if they are just patient and understand the struggle, Communism (dictatorial socialism) will triumph as the wave of the future.

Stupidly, year after year, decade after decade and, generation after generation American education, American money and the American press continued to support a completely failed social philosophy. A totalitarian ideology that can exist only by force and deceit on the fallacious spoon-fed belief that such a system will become less violent. The same assumption has been made about "NOW".

FEMINISTS, as they get older and less satisfied by a philosophy that doesn't work, will become more filled with self-pity and in turn will be increasingly shrill in their petty demands and wants.

For every, average educated woman, black or white, orange, yellow or green that enters the already totally inefficient American work force, there is one less possible job available for the average black American male.

Why? Because the average black American male is the least likely employable individual; having far less reading, writing and arithmetical skills at even the simplest level of clerical opportunity.

Heavy American industry is a thing of the past. The American Public School System has been such a miserable failure of late (at least the last fifty years) that the average black American male is economically and functionally in deep trouble.

Black American women who have been seduced by the FEMINIST movement would have better served themselves, their community and their men had fought their political and educational leaders, demanding a decent education and law enforcement system within their own neighborhoods. Instead, many of these same women actually enlist black American males to participate in their own economic demise - another grand triumph of "NOW".

When magic wands are raised by FEMINISTS and politicians to create tens of millions of unnecessary jobs mostly in government and some in industry, America simply becomes more inefficient and industrially non-competitive - a minor inconvenience to be ignored by ranting FEMINISTS as they screech for more opportunity and more pay!

"NOW" has a Gloria mentality," . . . great in emergencies, but can't handle everyday life." Somebody forgot to tell little Gloria and her girlfriends that when everything gets so screwed up by "NOW's" demands, Everyday becomes an emergency!

American FEMINISTS have lied to themselves, their followers and to the American public. What, you might ask constitutes a lie? According to Webster's unabridged, second edition, 1979:

> "1. To utter falsehood with the intention to deceive;
> also to utter falsehoods habitually."
> "2. To cause an incorrect impression; to present a

misleading appearance; to deceive one; as figures frequently lie."

Do yourself favor, **READ Friedan's "Feminine Mystique".** List all the ills she blamed on mothers staying at home. Then list her prognostications regarding the effect "college educated" career FEMINISTS would have, inciting an American Communist Revolution. If she was right, join "NOW"!

But if, as is the truth, she was absolutely wrong then any support whatsoever you give the FEMINIST movement is based upon nothing but lies. Big, institutionalized lies that have been repeated over and over again until perceived as the truth. Any buoyancy in the American economy is due to technology and overwork of the employed, while the poor suffer immeasurably.

It is incumbent upon honest people to correct one's opinion or beliefs upon discovery of falsification of information, to do otherwise is the same as to intentionally continue to practice deceit and bear false witness. The truth is:

- Africans practiced slavery thousands of years before there was such terminology as white Anglo-Saxon males. **Africans continued to practice slavery years after it was outlawed in America.**

- There are no white Anglo-Saxon males (Oh! maybe 4 or 5 in a cave somewhere).

- Starting cars whose batteries are run down does not constitute one of life's great emergencies.

- The mere fact that one requires masturbation to satisfy one's own sexual gratification does not automatically designate a second party as responsible for one's own lack of spontaneity.

- Nine room homes occupied by loving women do not qualify as concentration camps.

- Sage Advice is wisdom obtained through successful completion of a task well done, with loving care. While having the good sense to sit back and enjoy a blissful respite while contemplatively reflecting on one's blessings, with malice toward none.

All that has passed for wisdom and intellectualism in the FEMINIST movement after over fifty-years of shrill rhetoric has collapsed by the sheer weight of accumulated evidence by any reasonable measure, statistical correlation, observation, government data, empirical knowledge or just plain old common sense.

The record since the inception of "NOW" is strewn with disaster after disaster, millions of wrecked lives, utter chaos and the resultant elevation of a group of stupid, indulgent, greedy women to near sainthood.

American FEMINISTS should be ashamed for enshrining such wimps and perpetuating their own lives filled with deceit. Here is an accurate mini-description of your latest heroines:

- Gloria, who went to Smith, whereupon she learned to write in the first person singular.
- Betty, who espoused a philosophy of scorched earth in a book that was completely wrong on every major premise. Yet, despite the verification of her falsehoods, millions of followers extol the merits of her obsolete and tattered, childish utterances.
- Margaret, who made up fairy tales, concocted from the fantasies of teenage native girls, and had the gall to call it anthropology.
- Jane, who from age 15 to 35 made herself throw up fequently, sometimes five to twenty times a day for twenty years. She had the nerve to promote exercise tapes on how to lose weight and along the way shilled for North Vietnam.

Either American FEMINISTS are just plain stupid or they just don't give a damn. Do you really want your daughters to emulate these women? Have you no minds of your own?

It's difficult to determine which are the sicker personalities, the leaders of "NOW" or their followers. Unfortunately, even women who are vocally opposed to the FEMINISTS on many issues rally to the cry of ERA and equal pay for equal work. There are buried somewhere within these two themes a kernel of truth.

A little truth "HYPED" by media can justify an otherwise totally warped view of reality! Cleverly contrived socially inept theories have always relied upon the strength of a few grains of popular truth to support an entire stable full of self-serving nonsense.

YOU'VE COME A LONG WAY BABY! Already, in fifty short years, you're further behind then when you started. You're still looking for an easy way out of the real world! What the hell! One fantasy is just as good as another. Unfortunately, in your latest one, poverty in old age is your Holy Grail, coupled with childless loneliness, in direct violation of your biological imperative.

But please girls, this time around, omit the fantasy of white Anglo-Saxon males as the dragons in your dreams. Lay your failures at the feet of some real bogey FEMINIST women. Hey! Here's a cute idea, next time around blame the five horses of the merry-go-round, Germaine, Betty, Gloria, Margaret and Janie!

XIII. WHAT "NOW" GIRLS?

Why, throughout the pages of this book, have I been so vitriolic in denunciation of "NOW" and the typical American FEMINIST? Because I really believe a mind is a terrible thing to waste. The instability of the mental gyrations of FEMINISTS has created untold mountains of human misery.

FEMINISTS, as no other group in history, have squandered enormous amounts of psychic energy. Under the guidance of vindictive, screwed up, narcissistic females they have wasted their lives whining over imagined injustices.

American men have a tendency to ignore, sympathize with or argue with these FEMINISTS on a low key, rational basis, engaging in endless, non-productive dialog. For the continued duration of such wasted effort, honest women as well as white Anglo-Saxon designated bogeymen suffered shameless outrages of interminable abuse. All this hysteria created from a bunch of silly, mixed up, harping, stupid self-proclaimed FEMINISTS.

ENOUGH is enough! The FEMINIST movement under the banner of "NOW" has shattered the lives of women, children and "minorities"; directing their efforts in such a manner that their energies have been exhausted battling non-existent bogeymen and conservative women.

The FEMINIST movement is "NOW" a self-evident farce. The measured results of its impact on American Society have culminated in absolute failure. American women and black men are "NOW", after fifty years, far worse off, both economically and psychologically because of the perpetuation of such garbage intellectualism.

It is not my intention to further dwell on the schizophrenic nature of "NOW" but rather to demonstrate how ridiculous it is. By such demonstration, American FEMINISTS can be freed of their purgatorial malaise of the seemingly unanswerable question, "What "NOW" girls?"

Before unmasking the duplicity of "NOW" in placing women on a battlefield of human misery with only internal conflict and stupidity as their weapons, **it is suggested that you actually read the books** cited earlier. Until such time as you do read their books, the chances are that you do not have a mind of your own.

You will remain a whining puppet of crazies who are bent on your own self-destruction. Such a minute display of independent intelligence might provide you with a modest amount of self-esteem and inner peace. Don't rely on others - THINK FOR YOURSELF.

There are an infinite number of possible avenues to investigate in attempting to recommend a course of action in the determination of one's chosen path in life, let alone self-direction for millions of confused, unhappy FEMINISTS.

Thanks to the perfidy of "NOW" it is quite simple to present to intelligent women several irrefutable parameters to substantiate that of all possible intelligent choices, FEMINISM is completely unacceptable to all but the stupid, the duplicitous and the mentally deranged.

Before proceeding with an explanation of your life choice parameters, there are a few statements to be understood regarding FEMINIST preoccupations that must be recognized for what they are.

- Expect no more from life than you have already given on a day in day out conscious level of honest effort.
- Recognize that you are petty and selfish if you believe without effort you are entitled to attention, privilege, love, appreciation or any similar special consideration not guaranteed by nature or promised by your God.
- If you spend more than thirty minutes in the morning creating the illusion of a beautiful exterior, you are a troubled, insecure individual.
- If you are abnormally frightened by the possibility of pain or the responsibility associated with childbirth, be certain that you do not bury your fears deep within your subconscious.
- Such deeply repressed fears become breeding ground for concocted, spiteful rationalizations for childlessness dreams of megabuck "Careers" and biasness in favor of abortion.

PARAMETERS OF CHOICE IN REFUTATION OF "NOW"!

Is belief in the Christian-Judeo ethic compatible with "NOW"? The answer is unequivocally - NO! If you are of sane mind and of the Christian Judeo ethic then you cannot be a supporter or member of "NOW". Why? The dichotomy of your interests is quite simple. You are bound by the written and universally accepted commandments of God given to Moses on the mountain.

THOU SHALT NOT MURDER!

Even "NOW" must admit the best of odds are fifty-fifty that either:

ABORTION BY CHOICE IS MURDER OR IT IS NOT!

Under such chance conditions of possibilities, no intelligent Christian-Judeo woman in control of her mental faculties (not insane) would gamble away her opportunity for blissful eternal life

135

on the fifty-fifty chance that she may either be an accessory to, or the perpetrator of mass murder!

Despite superficial rationalizations to the contrary, the kindest of just Gods would not succumb to the forgiveness of such self-serving duplicity with the reward of blissful everlasting life, in direct and continued disobedience to his own commandment.

For Christian women there is an additional admonishment of Jesus:

"WHATSOEVER YOU DO TO THE LEAST OF MY
BRETHREN YOU DO TO ME!"

The choice of the sane, intelligent Christian-Judeo woman is clear and simple, either you are a believer or you are not. No negation of such choice can be obscured by the contrived arguments to the contrary by individual priests, Imams or rabbis. After all, what does he have to lose?

It's your immortal soul, not his, mine or theirs. No sane Christian, Jewish or Muslim woman would shoot craps with the stakes being eternal damnation or deprivation from the coming paradise.

Should American women of religious conviction choose to abide by their faith, they must immediately refrain from any endorsement of the principles of the FEMINIST movement; abandon the trivialities of FEMINIST' strictly showcase inducements with which they have baited the trap of your possible eternal damnation.

Having presented Christian-Judeo inclined FEMINIST activists and tacit supporters with a clear, intelligent choice as to their personal best interest, it remains for them to choose, but choose they must, or be declared mentally incompetent and/or complete hypocrites

Those who choose to remain in the ranks of "NOW", other than the stupid and insane, by definition are committed to a way of secular life that does not believe in any cause-effect relationship between this life and another existence.

Such women, as befits their philosophical choice, are entitled to believe and do anything that is not punishable by authority in this life, without compromising their convictions. Punishment by

136

authority, in and of itself, is not necessarily a consideration, only an unpleasant possibility that such a philosophical position would in one's self-interest attempt to avoid.

It is precisely these American FEMINISTS who have been most deceived by "NOW". Their world by definition is only comprised of this life and it is in their best interest to seek maximum pleasure and enjoyment through intelligent choice with the minimum amount of inconvenience or risk.

Even to the most hard core, anti-male, childless oriented FEMINIST, given the license to freely choose her best individual path in life, "NOW" would be faced with this same simple truth, even excluding the abortion issue.

The idea of a "Career" for the average American woman based upon factual evidence is absolutely ridiculous! The possibilities for "Career" opportunities in the American work force are all but statistically non-existent. There are not, nor have there ever been, "Careers" for 98% of American men; let alone women.

American labor is geared to jobs, not "Careers". For that small percentage of "Career" opportunities, one must devote seventy to one hundred hours per week over a period of thirty to fifty years. Except for the minimum of respites, such a path of success is inseparable from one's life. Even in opportunities afforded a very small segment of the population, one must run the risk of having the best-laid plans of mice and FEMINISTS go astray.

If a FEMINIST sets out to pursue a "Career", in lieu of marriage and children, she will almost certainly become just another failed statistic, a poor elderly matron, for whom nobody gives a damn. She will have only herself and "NOW" to blame.

For those very few talented, lucky or cunning women who obtain "Career Success", even they should consider the quality of life inherent in devoting thirty to fifty years running an automotive company, doing commercials for Pepsi Cola or programming suspect managerial programs for computer applications.

Because of female bias within our social structure, only the female has a choice to forego or postpone active participation in the work force. This gives her the opportunity to take advantage of all the opportunities of maintaining her lifestyle options without committing herself to an irrevocable course of action.

An American FEMINIST adhering to the dictates of "NOW", by force of peer pressure, and because of the limited duration of her biological reproductive time span, eliminates all her options.

The intelligent, secular, American FEMINIST has eminently more opportunity for an enriched, pleasurable life if she is well educated, develops marketable skills, marries a hard working male and has one or more offspring. Having established a strong foundation of learning, security and family relationships, she can explore numerous lifestyle objectives without totally committing herself to a lifetime of loneliness and poverty.

If you are a loving single woman who truly enjoys being unmarried or a loving lesbian, each with malice towards none then the following does not apply to you.

Total heartbreak awaits the "Career" FEMINIST who discovers, the hard way, what older generations of intelligent women already intuitively knew. Working in American industry all your life ain't fun!

Having achieved even a minimal base of learning, financial and family security, the intelligent woman is ready to explore those activities and creative lifestyles that offer her the best opportunity for earthly fulfillment at the least possible risk. Even less intelligent and/or poverty stricken women create the best possible average life insurance policy by acquiring a husband and nurturing at least one child.

Such a deliberate choice is less risky than an almost assured gruesome old age of loneliness. On a purely intelligent, rational, opportunistic level of choice, such an approach to a purely secular life is in your best interest.

You see FEMINISTS, you can always abandon or at the very least divorce yourself from carrying out your responsibilities or charade, if you so choose. But you have placed yourselves in an advantageous position. You keep open all your options without risking everything on the statistically poor possibility of a "Career". Who knows, you might even fall in love and discover parenthood is a beautiful adventure?

There are those who, out of stupidity, will remain hard core nonsensical adherents to the self-defeating grandiose fantasies of "NOW". These are the very same FEMINISTS who will depend upon their duplicitous natures to similarly attempt to seduce their own creator in the next life, should one exist.

With a FEMINIST, no sacrifice of yours is too great to satisfy her minute by minute gratification of her every imagined whim! FEMINISM is a chosen way of life of fanciful preoccupation with self; even to the extent of pursuing an irrational course of action in opposition to one's own best interest.

Feminists simply cannot tolerate the realities of their own existence!